Sangrar lo

The first time I met him I was thirteen, a freshman in high school. I was the new girl at Conard High School in West Hartford, a suburb in Connecticut. I transferred in during the middle of the school year. I received my first dose of culture shock when I walked the hallways that first day. My eyes could not process the number of white students I saw in one place at the same time. *I could go snow blind here.* My old high school, also in Connecticut, was a sea of brown and black faces with droplets of white here and there. I am, for sure, going to keep out of trouble in this school, I think to myself as I stare wide eyed at a girl rushing past me. She is sporting green, spiky hair and neon pink high-top sneakers.

I report to the main office and meet with a guidance counselor, an old fragile woman with a pale face. She looks so ancient that I am scared she is going to drop dead right in front of me. *Goodness help me, I was never trained in CPR.* She stares at me as if I am being a nuisance to her on her very hectic day. I can almost hear crickets chirping as we stare at each other in silence.

She breaks the awkward silence as she cackles, "Just waiting on a student to come and show you our school."

I scan the recruitment posters on her wall for colleges in the area; Central Connecticut State University, University of Connecticut, University of Hartford, Trinity College. No pretty shiny laminated community college posters. I do not get any guidance at all about classes, expectations, my future endeavors or higher education. Don't think she fits the title of a "guidance" counselor much.

I am relieved when a friendly cinnamon kissed face walks into the office. Like a hawk, she swoops into the office, grabs my book bag, shakes my hand, and gently yanks me out of the stuffy, mothball fragranced office.

"See you later Mrs. Blanca, I will take good care of her!"

She hasn't said a word to me yet and I like her already. *"Hola, buenos dias.* I will be your tour guide for today. Oh and by the way don't listen to anything Mrs. Blanca just said, she's older than Mark Twain and gets nervous around people like us. I'm Yvette." She turns to notice that I am staring inquisitively at the students walking by who are all staring at me with equal curiosity.

As we walk down the hall Yvette breaks down the politics behind the town I just moved to with my dad. I was originally from Stratford, a town in southern Connecticut. She tells me how half of the people in this school live on the other side of West Hartford in fenced in houses, with housekeepers and gardeners, while the other fifty percent, like her family, live in modest houses and apartments and work as gardeners. She mentions the kids who live in Hartford that sneak across the border into the West Hartford school system because it is ranked one of the top schools in the state. *Like refugees from Cuba minus the floating rafts, sunburn and dehydration.* The best of the best, neighbors with the worst of the worst.

Little do I know that I just met the guiding light who would be my pillar of strength in my trials and tribulations in years to come.

"Umm do you speak de English? You was born on the island?"

I stutter, "The island...Long Island? No. Uhhh I was born in New York?"

Apparently, Mrs. Blanca had asked her to be a guide for a new girl who was coming from Puerto Rico. Yvette laughs as she says, "She still thinks that I'm a Puerto Rock, I get the feelin' she don't give a shit where my family is from." She chuckles as she turns around and points to a huge Dominican flag patch sewn to her backpack. "To her, we all in the same banana boat headin' in the same direction." She grins, sounding like a geography teacher as she reports, "You know Hartford has the highest percentage of people with Puerto Rican ancestry in the continental United States? I think there's more Ricans here than on the island. That's why they think we all from the *same* island."

I tell her that my family is from Peru. Before she can even ask, I reply, "It's the country next to Colombia." She nods her head in silence, acknowledging the fact that she has no idea where Peru is. *Story of my life.* Sometimes I feel like I popped out from a figment of my imagination. *Like Frodo and the Shire.* I never met another classmate from Peru or even anyone who could point to it on a map, at the very least. I always imagined what it would be like to sit in a classroom surrounded by people who grew up like me. With people who didn't go home and eat rice and beans every day like the mass majority of Puerto Ricans I grew up with. With people that were not terrified of the letter *R* when they spoke Spanish. But that would never be a reality, unless I moved to Peru, and I didn't see that happening any time soon.

Technically, I am from New York but my roots are buried deep in Peru. People would always inquire, "So where you from?"

"New York."

"No, but where you *really* from?"

"Port Chester."

The precise question should have been, "What nationality are you?" but when you are thirteen articulation is not abundant.

"Ladies, where you headed?" We both quickly turn to see a tall skinny black man wearing a wrinkled, faded security guard uniform in a shade of was-black-a-long-time-ago. He is sporting a railroad track smile with every other tooth missing as Yvette says, "Joel, this is a new student her name is… oh, I never got your name!"

"Adeline… Ady," I reply, loud enough so I won't have to repeat my name again. I have also never met another person with the same name as me (besides my grandmother who I was named after).

"…I was just bringin' her around, and I have lunch next period, so now I'm just showin' her where to meet me after her class, so that she don't get lost, since this is her first day. You know stuff like that type…" It is clear from the way she is rambling that we are not where we are supposed to be.

"You betta get in there 'fore Kavorkiam find you Yvette, you already got Saturday detention 'cause a him. Now get, 'fore he roll 'round here lookin' for someone to snatch up." He starts directing us into the cafeteria like one of those people who directs airplanes on the runway.

As we make our way inside to the lunch line she gossips, "That's Joel. He's one of three security guards we got here. He always got our back. A few months ago, one of the biggest dealers in the school got snitched on and was 'bout to get arrested. The cops got here to search his locker but Joel snuck into his locker and hid a HUGE stash few minutes before cops got to it. Joel kept it all for himself but he still saved his ass."

Yvette inconspicuously grabs two bags of chips and throws them in her book bag as she walks by the lunch lady at the cash register. I follow her as we walk out to the cafeteria. It feels like all eyes are on me; I really hate being the center of attention.

Yvette throws smiles and waves to a few people like a beauty pageant queen until we reach a table towards the back where she plops down on the edge of the seat, long curly locks bouncing along with her. Yvette is a big girl, not a fat girl, but a *Dominicana* with curves. We are the complete opposite. She has a golden brown complexion while my skin is fair, long gold tight curls while mine is black and bone straight and curves where I am a skin and bones. *A modern day Olive Oil.*

As she introduces me to a group of colorful faces I feel my nervousness float away. I feel like I have been holding my breath since I walked into the school and now I was able to breathe again. As silly as it sounds, I had felt like I was going to be the only Hispanic in a school of white people. Don't get me wrong, I had white friends growing up and I even dated a cool white boy for a while, but there is something to be said about being in the absence of *any* minorities that made me nervous.

We sit down with the crew as Yvette throws me a bag of chips. She tells me she lives in a small house that her father is able to afford because he is a successful DJ at a local Spanish radio station. *La Gigante, WRYM 840 AM!* She doesn't get into details but she obviously has harsh feelings towards her father. Yvette lives in the house with her mom, dad, three sisters, younger brother, two year old niece, and the ghost of the former homeowner (he opens the oven door all the time). Her house is always occupied, she has never in her life been in her house alone.

As the bell rings I see some people from our table leave and notice that there is a big group of students coming in for the first lunch wave. When I ask Yvette if we should be leaving, she grins, "Do you know what class you suppose' to be in right now?"

I pull out a printed schedule from my backpack. Yvette glances at it, crumples it up, and tosses it in a nearby trash can. She smiles again and repeats, "Do you know what class you suppose' to be in right now?"

"Guess not," I offer as I'm thinking again about keeping out of trouble.

"Let's be out."

It is still warm out and the sun is beaming its New England shine. As I take in the fresh air, I abruptly get a lung full of cigarette smoke. We turn the corner and are greeted by a lineup of smokers on the metal bleachers. *Bleacher Creatures lined up line a chain gang.* Yvette introduces me to a few people in the crowd referring to me as "the new girl from San Juan". Both of us laughing, she pulls out a pack of cigarettes from her bra and offers me one.

Writing this now, I wish I could write that I declined the offer but I was a casual smoker already by then. I always thought that those cheesy commercials about peer pressure and smoking were totally off point, but in a sense they do ring true. If everyone else around you is doing it, you are more likely to do it too. At least you didn't see us sitting around huffing glue. Teenagers have to make choices: some good, some bad.

Both with cigarettes in hand, we take a seat on the bleachers away from the crowd. "So what's your deal Ms. Puerto Rico, why you end up in West Hartford out of all places? It's so boring here."

"I started out this year at Stratford High, my freshman year and I got booted out within a few months." I offer with a little smirk, "I don't know, I just ended up here because my dad."

I think back about my continuous trouble at Stratford High for skipping classes, mouthing off to teachers and leaving school grounds. After being caught smoking weed in the girls bathroom the principal quietly kicked me to the curb. In true teenage form I told my mom he was lying and he just had it in for me. I lasted less than a month at a Catholic school and somehow found friends there that were worse than the ones in Stratford High. My stepfather made it very clear that he didn't like paying for private school for a kid who didn't appreciate it. That was the point where my mom told me that it would be a good idea for me to go live with my father "for a little while".

I was living with my father within a week of my mom's decision. I didn't make a big deal out of the whole transition. I was in a transition already anyways, starting my adolescence on the wrong foot. By thirteen I was smoking weed, drinking, and being rebellious, and overall I just had a shitty attitude. At the time, I rationalized that my home life was reason enough to act out and do what I pleased.

My parents had moved from Peru to Spain with my two older brothers years before I was born. They were searching for opportunity and success they couldn't find in Peru and they already had family that was established in Spain. When Spain seemed to be a dead end they decided to go to their second option, New York. *Los Estados Unidos, donde los suenos conviertan en realidad!* So my mom made the journey with only the essentials, her two little boys, and a baby on the way, while my father stayed behind in Pamplona for a year while he finished his associate degree at the local college.

Nine months pregnant and in a strange new country, my mom found comfort in the universal language of food. She visited the local Carvel every day and eventually tasted every flavor of ice cream they had. Living in a small cramped apartment with her aunt she knew that she would have to find a place to stay before I arrived. Being the resourceful person she is, my mother used her basic elementary English to make a deal with the owner of Carvel to work in exchange for a crappy vacant apartment on top of the store.

When you grow up in a third world country you learn how to be resourceful in every situation. You have to learn how to use your surroundings to your advantage when you have very little to choose from. As a baby, my mother's crib was actually an old milk crate her mother skillfully decorated with reclaimed fabric. It was as beautiful as any bassinet you can buy nowadays in the store. Mami's toys were salvaged odds and ends that brought her and her siblings hours of fun. Her favorite pastime was playing with broken tiles with colorful designs that she used to trade with her friends like baseball cards.

Making the transition from life in South America to North America was difficult for my mom but she was used to change. She was a chameleon. Living in a strange new place, my mom made the transition as only she could: FUN. She took full advantage of the opportunities around her and explored New York with my two older brothers. Armed with a bus pass and a camera they discovered this new land like Pizarro (minus the killing, pillaging and trickery).

Just like clockwork, within two weeks of arriving they moved three huge suitcases into their new one bedroom apartment just as I came into the world. I narrowly escaped being born a Spaniard. Not that it would have been a bad fortune but my life story would not have been the same. I was born the first day of summer of 1980, I share that birthday with Prince William. We would be forever bound in my mind by our birth-dates as well as unforeseen tragedy in both our lives.

After juggling a part time job, a newborn, and two very energetic boys, my mom was relieved when my father joined us after my first birthday. During the early 80's there was a mass migration of people moving from New York to the suburbs of Connecticut. The cost of living was not only cheaper in the suburbs but there were more job opportunities. That is when we moved to Stamford, Connecticut. My father was able to secure a job as a mechanic, fixing machines for minimum wage. My parents found a nice duplex in a quiet area and were working their way towards "The American Cream" (making that money). My father would take pictures of us in the park or in front of our duplex with a white picket fence and send them home to Peru as a testament that we were making it.

I have vague memories of playing in the park with my father and two brothers, or arts and crafts with my mother. At an early age I began to read and write short stories and I would bind the loose-leaf papers with yarn. We were not rich but I was given luxuries that my parents didn't have. I had a collection of Care Bears that I took care of like my own children. As I got ready for bed I would line my Care Bears around my bed and fall into a secure slumber. I never went to bed hungry.

******

Miles away in Hartford, he was lying in his bed in his Thundercats pajamas with hunger pains and a constant fear of windows shattering again in his bedroom from stray gunshots.

******

The story of my childhood is interrupted by a quick shout from someone running by, "Heads up 5-O is comin'!" Yvette pulls me into a nearby bathroom. I hide in one of the stalls and start to giggle. I laugh when I get nervous.

"Hey crazy, what you laughing at?" Yvette whispers from the next stall. She pops her head over the stall divider as she stands on the toilet and stares down at me.

"Nothin'. I just think I'm going to like this school," I murmur shrugging my shoulders, smiling.

She smiles back and hands me her pack of cigarettes. "Here hold these, just in case. You have an innocent face." I stuff them into my pocket and we wait for a few minutes until it seems safe.

Making our way back to the cafeteria we find a new group of people sitting at our table. One of them put my book bag on the dirty floor and was sitting in my chair.

They stare at me with amused looks until Yvette introduces us. "This is Ady. Ady this is Emilio, Luis and Cutty." Under her breath she adds, "Cutty's the one that Joel saved from getting arrested."

Annoyed, I pick my book bag off the ground, dust it off and proclaim, "Hey, can I have my seat back?" Being the new girl I needed to establish that I was cool but also not one to be reckoned with.

"Uh, no." Cutty replies nonchalantly in a patronizing tone. This guy is wearing a ridiculously huge leather jacket despite the fact that it is a warm spring day. His jeans are draping off the chair they are so big on his skinny frame and his bottom jaw sticks out with an unsightly under bite like the Tin Man. Moving or not, I was getting my seat back.

"Okay." I plop down on his lap as if he is the chair, glance back, and give him a fake smile.

"Where you move from?" Emilio interrogates with a smile from across the table.

"Stratford." If Emilio isn't a drug dealer he must have a really good job. He is dressed head to toe in Karl Kani and is wearing a ridiculously huge gold chain with a pendant as big as his hand.

His wrist is weighed down with a monstrous matching gold bracelet. He has enough gold to rival Atahualpa's ransom (Peruvian history, look it up).

"I drive by there all the time when I go to New York." Before I can respond the third guy, Luis, says it is time to go. Dressed similar to the other two, Luis looks like a more muscular version of Cutty. *The Puerto Rican Musketeers: all for one, none for all.*

Grabbing his huge, clunky, grey cell phone off of the table, Cutty taps my shoulder as I lock eyes with Emilio. "Excuse me, can I have my legs back sweetie?"

As I get up Emilio grabs my hand. "Nice meeting you Ady, hope to see you soon, *amor*. Peace," he utters as he gives me a quick wink. My cheeks turn bright red. Of course, I had no way of knowing then as he walked out of that cafeteria door that he would be my destiny, my future… my husband. I also would have never predicted that the guy next to him would be locked up in twenty years for kidnapping, sexual assault and possession of narcotics with intent to sell.

After they leave, Yvette gives me the scoop on Emilio. "Girl, he's a player, he always got some girl on the side. He's cute, but he's trouble."

"Oh, he's taken?" I question, already curious about him from our very brief encounter.

"He just started messing with Maya, that girl over there that's staring at you." She points with her chin to another table. Maya is standing next to a table with a group of girls and they are all staring in our direction. She is wearing a black mini skirt with high white knee socks and a white button down shirt. She looks like a china doll, her skin is flawless. Her jet black hair is up in a bun but you can tell that it must be long and bone straight.

"Chinese chick?"

"Oh don't let her hear you say that, she will definitely give you shit, she's from Laos not China. Her and her sisters don't even associate with Chinese people; all their friends are Laotian, Puerto Rican or Black."

"This is my first day here, I'm not trying to get in trouble yet. Let's get outta here 'fore she starts some shit." I quickly snatch up my book bag.

We go to the main office and pick up another schedule. Yvette walks me to my art class and we exchange numbers.

"We going to chill later, call me if you want to go!" she yells when she is halfway down the hall.

As I walk in late to my art class my cheeks grow crimson as the teacher with fiery red hair notices me and welcomes me in a loud voice. "Everyone, attention, attention please! I would like you to welcome a new student to our class. This is Adeline Yllanes."

I politely smile as she butchers my last name. I hate it when people pronounce the "anes" in my name "anus"; it just sounds gross.

"We are already halfway through a project so if you just want to team up with someone for now... "

"She can help me," I hear a familiar voice call out. My stomach does back flips as I see Emilio smiling up at me.

I walk towards his table and he pulls an empty chair closer to his, and that was the start of what would become an awkward relationship between us.

I attend all my other classes curious about what this new place and new people will bring. As I wait in the front of the school at the end of the day to be picked up by my step mother, I see Maya and Emilio walking hand in hand. My stepmother pulls up and I dive into the car, exhausted. *"¿Como estas bebita, como te fue?"*

"Okay" I murmur, not in a mood to talk. I look out the window most of the ride home giving one word answers to Lorena's attempts at making conversation.

Lorena is the only skeleton in my father's closet. Growing up, everyone believes that their parents can do no wrong. Papi is a do-gooder who always does what is almost saintly. He always wears his seatbelt, doesn't test the speed limit and always uses his turn signals (even when no one is behind him). He is the type of person who will go into the bank and return money if he finds someone before him forgot to take it out of the ATM (yes, he actually did that before). He is against stealing cable or lying to the government to get assistance. He plays everything in his life by the rules, except for Lorena...

We pull up to Brittany Farms, an apartment complex in New Britain, the next town over from West Hartford. We were actually moving to West Hartford in five months but the house we were moving to wasn't even built yet. So after a lot of fighting with the board of education, Papi finally got permission to have me start out in Conard even though I should have been attending New Britain High School. It is true, tiny decisions can ultimately change the course of your future.

I can picture myself attending New Britain High School and getting lost in the chaos. N.B.H.S. is an overcrowded and underfunded prison disguised as a school. Forget about receiving any type of education besides sex and drug education. The only ones that made it out alive were the students in honors classes. You need different parts of an equation to equal success. I had 20 percent parental involvement, 20 percent healthy learning environment, 20 percent stable home atmosphere. I was just missing that 40 percent of individual determination, though I would find it eventually hidden somewhere beneath the earth. But at 14, I was not thinking about the future, I was in the here and now. And right now, I was being annoyed by a super skinny, hyper, irritating seven year old.

"Get out my face Guille," I scowl, trying to reach my room.

Guillermo, Guille for short, is the most annoying little seven year old I have ever encountered, who I currently share a room with. He is constantly bothering me and I guess I annoy him too. He is Lorena's son from a previous marriage. Before I moved in it was just him, his mom, and my dad. When I moved in it must have disrupted his stable world.

"How was your first day of school? Did you make any friends or did you cry in the bathroom?" he teases not waiting for an answer while jumping on his bed.

I kick off my shoes and change into jogging pants. I am tired, hungry and cranky. I wander into the kitchen and find a delicious banquet covering the stove. Lorena prepared *Aji de Gallina*, which literally translated means "Spicy Hen". It sounds gross and looks gross (exactly like puke) but it melts in your mouth and tastes like heaven. Shredded chicken in a creamy Peruvian sauce. Lorena serves me a plate over white rice and boiled potatoes. My mouth watering, I shovel it into my mouth and move in for seconds.

"Bebita, I don't know where you put all that food, you are so skinny." She teases with her slight accent. Lorena grew up in Peru with a strict mom and an even stricter father. Her father was a military man whose wife soon left him taking Lorena, her sister and brother far away. Being raised by a single mother was taboo in Peru so as soon as she got a chance Lorena left. She was courted by an Yllanes and the rest was history or so it would have been...

I throw my empty plate in the sink and retreat to my room. In my own world, I snuggle under my blankets and close my eyes. I can hear Guille playing outside with the neighbors. Grateful for a little peace and quiet, I take my daily nap. I love sleep, I truly believe that sleep is a gift from the Gods. What else can rejuvenate you and feel as good as taking a nap? After about an hour, I am refreshed and I decide to call Yvette and see if we can meet up. I don't see my pants with her number in the pocket. I left my jeans on the floor in the middle of the room before I went to eat and now the room is spotless. Oh no....

Lorena is a clean freak. If she isn't cleaning, she is nagging me to clean. She takes pride in maintaining an orderly household. I go into the living room and find her on the couch folding clothes.

She looks up, "*¿Oh, ya estas despierta?* Come."

She doesn't sound mad, content almost. We walk outside to the back where all the kids are playing. She sits down on a huge rock and motions for me to sit. The sun is setting and the kids are screaming, exhausting all their energy before they get locked up for the day.

"So how was school today?" she inquires while pulling out the pack of cigarettes I was holding for Yvette. She lights one up and hands it to me very casually as if we do this all the time. I don't know what to do. Do I take it, do I refuse, or do I explain that they aren't mine? If she wants to embarrass and confuse me, it works. I decide to refuse as I gently shake my head no while looking down at the ground.

"School was okay. I made a friend, Yvette, she's Dominican, super cool."

"*Que bueno.* Just make sure that you are making the right kind of friends *bebita*. For you to get a good education we are moving to West Hartford, just for you. We could off stay right here in New Britain until Guille starts high school but you know your father. He wants -*we* want the best for you. You have a wonderful chance to start fresh here. The problems that you were having in the past, you can leave in the past. We love you and we expect you to be a success. You have a future you have to ponder about. You are the only one that can create who you are going to be." She finishes the cigarette and puts it out on the rock we are sitting on. She throws the rest of the pack in a nearby trashcan. As she gets up to go inside she yells over her shoulder, "And tell Yvette she shouldn't be smoking Newport's, *le hace sangrar los pulmones!*"

Produce with Potency

The average person has 1,500 dreams a year. I, on the other hand, have double that because I love sleep. I can fall asleep anywhere. Yes, I am the person who will come over your house to visit and end up falling asleep comfortably on your couch while you tip toe around me. I always have a recurring dream/nightmare that I vaguely remember. I am going down an escalator, it is always the same escalator and I am always by myself. I have an anxious feeling that I am looking for something. As I look down for that something, I see that my left hand is swollen and looks like it belongs to King Kong. This feeling of anxiety mixed with the heaviness of my cartoon-like hand always makes me wake up and reach for my left hand as I try to shake off that weird sensation. The next morning I lay in my bed awake with my eyes closed.

My dad walks into the room, "*¿Princessa estas despierta? Ya es hora de listar,*" he whispers, bending down to give me a kiss on the forehead, he leaves as quietly as he came in. My father is the quietest, most tranquil person I have ever encountered. He walks as light as a feather and speaks like a small breeze feels.

I get up to go to the bathroom and find that Lorena beat me to it, so I go back to my bed and get under my warm covers while I wait for her to finish. I stare at the bed next to mine. I am glad for the early mornings when Guille is still sleeping. I like him best when he is not awake, he looks like an angel. His skin is almost translucent he is so white and his hair is jet black. He looks exactly like a ventriloquist doll. He really isn't that bad, he just bothers me all the time. He is actually a bright little kid, smart and inventive. However, I still have the urge to push him off the bed as he sleeps.

After a quick shower I get dressed and sit down to a breakfast of warm bread and avocados. I spread the avocado on the bread and top it off with Adobo and black pepper.

"*Beba*, I have to stay late at work today. I have to cover another floor." Lorena is a translator at Hartford Hospital. She was able to secure this job soon after coming to Connecticut.

"Don't worry, I can stay after school or go to the mall until you get out." I hope Yvette doesn't have plans already, I think to myself.

"Thank you, *provecho*," I mumble after wolfing down my breakfast. I am not going to be skinny much longer if I keep eating like this. It wasn't that my mom didn't feed me, there was always food in the house, it's just that I wasn't in the house much. I didn't want to face what happened to my mom. When I think of my mom I see two people, the mom I grew up with and the stranger who came and stayed with us while I was a teenager.

The mom I grew up with was a vibrant happy person who always kept her children busy. My brothers and I would constantly be in dance, theatre, violin or karate classes. At home we didn't sit in front of the TV very often. We would be occupied with art projects, cooking, or out in the backyard playing. Mami was always happy, smiling and laughing. We would create gingerbread houses from scratch for Christmas. I have a vague memory of sitting down to an Easter breakfast when I was little with hard boiled eggs dyed pink, blue, and yellow. She was fun and creative. That was the mom that I could remember, the one that I desperately tried to hold on to while the other mom snuck quietly into the house one night.

Mami had admitted to me, rather embarrassed, that she was attracted to Joseph in the beginning because he seemed to have what Papi didn't. He had success, defined by money and properties. That was what brought them together... real estate. Again, it is true that tiny decisions can ultimately change the course of your future. Joseph had a house to rent and Mami and Papi were looking for a place to stay. After a failed attempt to drive cross country to live in California we were almost homeless. We packed up almost all our belongings and got as far as Tennessee before we ended up upside down on the freeway with shattered glass everywhere. We still have a dented coffee mug somewhere that says WE CRASHED IN TENNESSEE. So we ended up back in Connecticut and Mami was working at the VNA in Danbury. She told me that Joseph was the supervising nurse on the floor and everyone hated him. He was arrogant, loud, and obnoxious; "disgusting" to quote Mami. He was renting an apartment in Bridgeport for dirt cheap, so Mami made a tiny decision to inquire about the apartment.

I don't remember exactly what happened next, and Mami and Papi have their own versions of the shift. This was how I remembered it: we packed up all of our things and moved into Joseph's apartment in Bridgeport. Mami, Papi, my two brothers and I were living on the first floor of a very nice house in a very dangerous area. It was like a juicy cherry sitting on top of a pile of shit. Mami claims her and Papi were having problems already and that Joseph had nothing to do with what happened next.

Our parents had decided that me and my brothers would go on a vacation during the summer break and visit our Uncle Lucho in Spain. I was seven years old and I'd never in my life spent a night away from my parents, and now I was leaving the country with my brothers. I missed my parents terribly the entire time and didn't want to go out much. My family in Spain tried to bring us out and make the best out of what would soon be an unfortunate reality when we got home. My brothers would bring down the big metal shutters in the house and tell me that it was time to go to bed at like six in the afternoon. They were teenagers and they wanted to go out and have fun and meet girls. I didn't blame them for not wanting to bring along their little sister, but for the longest, I thought the sun set earlier in Spain than the rest of the world.

After almost two months in Spain we came home to the fact that our parents were divorced. I didn't realize what divorce meant or how that affected our family but I did notice that Papi was no longer living with us. Papi moved out of the house quiet as a whisper and soon after, Joseph moved in as noisy as a locomotive. Joseph played guitar and grew up eating hamburgers and beef stew. I believe that Mami fell in love with his role as an "All American Guy". She grew up in Peru listening to the Beatles and watching American movies on the big screen and now she was married to that apple pie image.

The marriage was doomed from the very beginning. While standing at the altar exchanging their vows Joseph loudly belched and farted as Mami's family looked on in embarrassment. We ended up with Joseph, the complete opposite of my father. He was as "green – go" as you can go. Soon after marrying, we moved to a house in a quiet little neighborhood in Stratford, Connecticut, right on the beach. This was where my brothers and I experienced the loss of my mother. Joseph grew up with two very Catholic, very Polish parents who picked on him constantly. He was born with a very serious case of hyperkeratosis that caused his hands and feet to look less than normal. With this strict upbringing and steady nitpicking I guess it stuck, because that is exactly what he did with Mami and my brothers.

We have home movies of the first few months of the marriage where Joseph videotaped the new house. While he walks around taping every room, you can hear talk where Joseph is dominating the conversation and he is blatantly disregarding Mami's comments about the house. Her happiness of having a new home was overshadowed by the fact that Joseph was talking over her. He had the tendency to point out her mispronunciation of words and he would play the fool and make pretend he didn't understand what she was trying to say.

After a few months of Joseph, my brother Danny had enough and moved in with Papi. My other brother, Moises, stuck it out a bit longer. His natural instinct to protect made him stay for the fight. To complicate matters even more, Mami found out that she was expecting soon after the marriage. Maybe if she didn't have my sister so soon after, she would have been able to pack up her bags and run as fast as she could the other way. I think by this time Mami realized to her horror that she was married to a monster; an All American Monster.

We were living in a beautiful house in a great neighborhood and I was attending a good school. It would have been ideal if Mami was happy but she wasn't, she was sad and trapped. Over the years Joseph's twisted personality took over my mother's identity. She was no longer the Mami that was smiling all the time; she tried to keep up her image for us but her glow slowly died out. My younger sister was all that kept her going and even she couldn't stop the other Mami from coming into our lives. Eventually, Mami turned to drinking and it soon spiraled into an uncontrollable addiction.

I was still young at the time she started; only about ten years old when she began her journey down that lonely, drunken road. I was slowly being forced to grow up and take care of my little sister, Chiara, when Mami was having her "episodes" in the house. I had to take on the responsibility of cooking, cleaning, taking care of my baby sister, and making sure Mami was safe. I would have to hide her car keys and try and talk her out of walking to the liquor store drunk. I had lost the mother that I grew up with and I blamed it all on Joseph. After a few years of being mini-mom I started getting tired of the whole situation. I was angry at my mom for not snapping out of her depression and getting better. I was annoyed that she couldn't get our things together and leave Joseph in the misery that he called normal.

By the time I was thirteen, I was beginning to resent the cards that I was dealt and had begun to turn my back on the possibility of ever having a secure home life. My anger (and adolescent hormones) took over and I began to lash out at everyone. I would skip school and go to friends' houses where we would drink or smoke. I slowly gave up on studying and going to classes. During this time I stayed away from home as much as I could. I wanted to shield my eyes from what was slowly turning into my dysfunctional life. I felt like I was trapped in a box and didn't have the tools to get out.

With all the trouble I was getting into, Mami decided that I had to change my environment. I was neutral about the decision of getting the boot except for the fact that I would be leaving my little seven year old sister behind. I practically raised Chiara and I was afraid of leaving her alone in the house with Mami and Joseph. I was torn between being relieved that I didn't have to play a teenage mother anymore and the fact that my sister wasn't coming with me. So with a torn heart, I left half of it with my sister and with the other half, I made the move to "Papi's World."

There I was with half a heart, a full stomach, and a new day full of possibilities. I give Lorena a goodbye kiss and glare at Guille with a forced smile. I walk outside where Papi is waiting for me in the car with the heat on making sure the car is warm for me. As I reach the passenger door he leans over and opens the door from his seat. I smile inside noticing all the little things that Papi does out of habit to make me feel special. I still have a chip on my shoulder but it is hard to be mean when you are in the presence of kindness.

"I thought you told Tio Lucho you were going to quit smoking," I blurt out, noticing the faint smell of cigarette smoke. Papi has been a smoker since the age of eleven!

"I told him I was going to try. I tried and it didn't work today. I will try again tomorrow *Princessa, te prometo*." He smiles at me with a half grin. "*¿Lorena te dijo que no te puede recoger después de las clases?*"

"Yeah, I told her that I was going to hang out with a friend anyways."

Papi works third shift so the only time I see him during the week is in the morning before school. He is a mechanic at Data Mail in Newington, where he fixes industrial machines. He is a hard worker who never calls out sick and is always on time; the true definition of a dedicated worker.

We ride the rest of the way in silence. Papi is the only person in the world who I can sit with in silence and not feel like we have to say something just to fill the void. It is a comfortable silence that only Papi could create for me.

"*Toma, para almuerzo.*" He offers, handing me a five dollar bill for lunch. "*¿Necesitas más?*"

"No, that's enough. Thanks Papi."

With Papi's face still fresh in my mind, I decide that I am going to try my hardest to make this day productive.

I attend all of my morning classes and reach lunch without any incidences. I have a minor situation in my English class but nothing major. I introduce myself to the ancient, pasty teacher, Mr. Casey, as he stresses the fact that I am coming in so late in the year. He loudly mentions to me how it would be hard for me to catch up, especially since English is my second language (he must have been gossiping with Mrs. Blanca). Laughing to myself,

I decide to hold my tongue, maybe I can milk it. As he stands in front of the class with his archaic suit and bow tie, his long, pointy white finger points to my name in his attendance book. He makes a half- assed attempt to pronounce my name.

"Is that how you pronounce it?" he questions loudly, as if I am hard of hearing. Red-faced and squirming at my desk with everyone staring at me, I jump out of my seat and walk to the blackboard. I spell out my name in huge exaggerated letters A-D-E-L-I-N-E - Y-L-L-A-N-E-S. I pronounce each syllable as if *he* were hard of hearing, staring at Mr. Casey in his unfriendly, cold, blue eyes.

"You're the *English* teacher right? You should know how to read." I sit back down and don't hear another thing he says for the rest of the class. He should be a master of phonetics:

A-S-S-H-O-L-E.

Stomach growling, I'm standing in the lunch line when Yvette pops up behind me. We walk to the same table we sat at the day before, where I see some new faces. I smile at no one in particular and sit down to wolf down my burger. *I'm starving!* As I devour my greasy hamburger and oily fries I feel someone staring at me. I looked around and notice a girl at the next table glaring me down.

The girl soon walks over to my table and asks me if I'm enjoying my lunch with a mug that says she wants to start trouble. She's dressed in all black and has huge hoop earrings and a gold three finger ring that looks like brass knuckles. *Ouch!* She is pale with jet black hair that is pulled back into a tight bun. She looks like she got dressed this morning to whoop ass. *This is a big ass girl!*

Not trying to make any enemies yet I retort, "Yeah, it's aight" I try to keep a neutral tone. I'm still famished and I really just want to finish my lunch with no altercations. Besides, if I have to go head up with this girl I am going to get my ass kicked for sure.

"Good, 'cause if I was hungry I would take your whole lunch," she growls, as she comes closer to my face.

Slowly realizing that this girl is trying to chump me, I spit out what I am still chewing on top of the uneaten portion of my burger and slowly slide the tray in her direction. "*Toma,* you can have it." As I stand up to face this huge girl I turn and see Yvette staring at me in horror. Now standing face to ...well, shoulders, the girl exclaims, "Bitch... you tiny but you got *cojones* huh?! I like that. What's your name?"

"Ady," I respond with an air of confidence and relief that I am not sprawled out on the floor right now, "want some fries?" I ask as a peace offering.

"Girl, you silly! I'm Nicki. Yvette, what up? We gonna chill after school today if you wanna roll," she comments as she puts her earrings back on.

"Cool, I'm not doing nothing and Ady's coming too." She poses more like a statement than a question.

"Strait," I chirp back happily.

The bell rings and I tell Yvette that I am going to class. I am trying to keep afloat in the fast current of white faces. There are one or two familiar faces from the lunch table but for most of my classes I am the only "His-panic" (I like dissecting words...HIS-PANIC, tell me that's not intentional). Sitting at my desk waiting for the teachers to start class I listen to the chatter, "Just got back from Cape Cod... we rented a cottage in Lake George it was so boring... I had to visit my dad...took me to Martha's Vineyard... feels guilty about the divorce... better buy me that Mercedes..." What?! These people definitely did not live on my planet, they seem like aliens to me. Do they even eat like I do? Do they breathe the same air I do? Do they put their clothes on the same way I do in the morning? *No, we gotta put our pants on twice as fast and do twice as much, in the same amount of time, to even get half the recognition they do.*

The highlight of my day is my art class when I get to see Emilio. "*Amor*, I haven't seen you all day. Where you been hiding? I was looking for you," he looks at me with a huge smile as I walk into the classroom.

The bell rings and Emilio walks me to my locker. I put away my crisp uncracked books and grab my book bag. Emilio pulls out a Sharpie and writes his number on the inside door of my locker.

"Where you going, want a ride?"

"Na, I'm good. I'm gonna chill with the girls."

Yvette and Nicki both give me that look when they see me walking up with Emilio.

"Don't ask," I admit as he disappears into the crowd.

"Anyways… let's be out." Nicki calls to a group of girls behind her.

Yvette introduces me to the other girls. "This is Lisa, she's the one that messes around a lot but she still my best friend," she jokes while wrapping her arm around her neck and giving her a hanging hug.

"Huh, *tu eres la puta!*" Lisa exclaims in perfect Spanish. She is ghost white with long bleach blonde hair and she's wearing a white t-shirt that shows off her ridiculously big boobs. She might be a white girl, but she has more junk in the trunk than Sanford and Son.

"This is Evelyn, she just moved here from New York." Yvette gestures towards a pretty, petite Puerto Rican girl with curly locks. She is light skinned with dark black hair, and she's wearing tight black jeans and an even tighter black and white striped blouse that leaves nothing to the imagination.

"Hey, I'm glad I'm not the new girl no more!" she squeals, sounding like Rosie Perez.

As we cross the parking lot I look at the students getting into their cars and I can't believe what they are driving. There are buckets in the lot too but the really nice cars stand out.

Curious, I ask Nicki, "Which one is yours?"

"Which what?" She looks puzzled.

"Which whip?" I clarify.

She starts laughing, "Oh no mama, we are trooping it! Don't one of us have a car."

"Oh, I don't either, I was just asking." Embarrassed that I made the assumption.

"I swear, when people find out you from West Hartford they think you rich and live in a big fucking mansion!"

"Oohh, were are definitely rich! I think Daddy has hundreds of thousands saved in a secret account that Mami doesn't know about. He never ever spends money and I know he is getting paid at the radio station. Watch, when he dies then, then, we gonna be rich." Yvette says with a scowl.

"Shiiiit, I wish I lived in a mansion. Or even one of these houses would be straight to live in." Evelyn points to one of the moderate homes that we are walking by. The street is lined with two story capes and ranch style homes. Well maintained and well-manicured lawns are the norm. "But I'm not complaining,

Hillcrest is strait, aint got hardly no roaches. But Amy snores up a storm and kicks all night! Had me falling asleep in class!"

"Guess I'm lucky, my little brother don't make no noise at night. He don't even move in his bed, it's like he's dead," I throw out.

"Oh you guys think that you are stereotyped because you live in West Hartford? Try being a white, Jewish girl who lives in West Hartford then tell me what people assume about you. After all these years, the neighbors still think we own the house that we are renting." Lisa offers.

We had been walking for a while when Lisa pulls out a pack of Newport Lights. She offers me one and I decline. I enjoy smoking but I never suffered from the addiction to smoke. I don't crave cigarettes and don't see the point in walking and smoking. You need to breathe in order to walk, right?

"Hey, you still got my pack of cigarettes?" Yvette turns to ask me.

"Oh, I forgot to tell you! My father's…my step-mom found them in my pocket!"

"Cigarettes are nasty anyways. If I am going to breathe anything into my lungs it better be a fat blunt." Nicki says while making pretend she has one in her mouth.

"I think bogies and weed are both nasty and I don't see how yall be smoking that garbage. You all going to be old ladies with cracked leather skin and nasty coughs. While me, I'm gonna be stealing your old wrinkled husbands cause I'm gonna still look fine." Evelyn starts shaking her booty as she walks as we all laugh.

We walk almost two miles, chatting about the day and the girls start asking me questions, curious about what I am about.

"Let's stop at my house first, I want to change." Nicki offers, turning the corner. "Lisa put that cigarette out my mom gonna have a fit if she sees you smoking in front of her house."

We walk up to a tiny blue house with a neglected lawn and a cracked driveway. "I'll be back," she says as she rushes into the house. We gather on the front porch and sit sprawled out on the stairs.

"Ady, how was your classes?" Yvette inquires.

"It was aight, borin'. I don't know, I don't really have no one to talk to yet. The people aren't mean or nothing, I just don't have anything to talk to them about. The teachers are all friendly with the other students like they chill on the weekends. I aint never seen so many white people in one place. No offence." I add as I look at Lisa to see her reaction.

"None taken. That's what you see when you look, a bunch of white people. What I see is a bunch of white people, with money. I don't have anything in common with half those people either. That's why I am stuck here chilling with you *sucias*." Lisa says playfully.

"So what nationality are you? You look Colombian." Evelyn interrogates me.

"No, I'm Peruvian," I say ready to explain myself again.

"Oh! Y'all eat that *cebiche* that is off the hook right? I use to live across the street from a Perubian restaurant in the Bronx. One time…"

Evelyn's voice trails off as we hear Nicki screaming inside the house. The screams are muffled but loud enough to hear through the closed door. As we all stand still trying to listen to what is happening a car pulls up in the driveway. A little boy jumps out of the car and runs over to the front door. He jumps over us and doesn't give us a second look. He goes inside for a second and then races back out to the car and screams, "Dad! Nicki is fighting with Mom again. I think you should tell her and her friends to leave."

A diesel, middle aged black man steps out of the car and stares in our direction with a mean look. We all stand up and quickly jump off the steps so that he can pass by. "Hello," he mutters as he passes into the house. "Nicki, I just got home and all I want to do is relax. You leaving?" We hear him bark.

Nicki swings open the front door and starts walking towards the street. "Come on, let's be out." She calls to us without looking back. As we start to follow her, a rather large white woman comes to the screen door. She is dressed in a floral muumuu and has rollers in her hair.

"Nicki, don't you fucking come back here if you don't got my money!" she shouts at the top of her lungs.

As we spill into the street we follow Nicki in silence for a while. The awkwardness of the scene still fills the air. We were all thinking the same thing but no one wanted to be the first one to ask what just happened.

Nicki finally breaks the silence as we walk down a side street. "Peep this, she been trying to charge me rent for the past few months. I told her I can't get a job 'til I'm sixteen that she needs to wait for another year and a half. She just don't understand. Where the fuck am I going to get 200 dollars a month?"

"Ah man. What does your Dad say?" I ask, picturing my father sitting back while Lorena asked me to pay rent. I flash back to this morning when Papi gave me lunch money and asked if I needed more. What kind of mother would ask their fourteen year old daughter to pay rent?

"Nothing. I wish my father could say something. He passed away when I was a baby. My *step*-father agrees with her. He says I gotta work for what I have. He look at me dirty when I grab something to eat in my own house." Yvette told me later that Nicki's mother was disowned when her parents found out that she was dating a *Poor-too Rican*. Nicki's father spoiled her mom with everything she ever wanted and even more when he found out that she was carrying his baby. He spent lavish amounts of money on her, all funded by a very big drug boom in the late seventies. But along with the money came the danger, too, and he was gunned down one night in Hartford, right in front of her mom while she was holding Nicki in her arms.

"Hold up. Let me call my house for a second before we walk to Manda's house." Yvette pulls a dime out of her pocket and runs to the payphone ahead.

We walk into a laundry mat and hit the vending machines for munchies. "Daddy will be home in like two hours so I have to be home by then," Yvette reports, "My dad doesn't let me hang out at all. He thinks I'm home right now 'cause my mom told him I was taking a nap. He is super strict with us." she whispers quietly. "It's because my older sister Vanessa got pregnant when she was thirteen. After that, me and the girls couldn't do shit anymore."

"Sucks for you," I sympathize.

We grab our barrage of junk food and start walking again. I am starving, so I dig into my Doritos and crack open my soda.

Nicki stuffs her cookies and chips into her book bag, "For later when I get the munchies." she says as if I should have known.

"Oh," I whimper looking down at my sad empty red bag. I imagined the girls sparking up a blunt and asking if I wanted to smoke. It has been exactly a week since I got high. My friends gave me a farewell bend off before I moved. A group of us went down to the beach and set up shop and partied until the morning. Walking home on the dark empty street, I saw no shame in what I was doing. I was at peace with myself when I smoked.

Marijuana is natural, it grows from the ground (I think my stepfather is even growing a few plants in his garden). When I drink, I don't get incapacitated like Mami does. Besides, a whole six pack of Zimas couldn't get me that drunk if I tried. Was I still that person that needed to mentally escape from her home life? I have only been living with Papi for a week but so far I had absolutely no complaints. When I used to come home high or drunk Mami would be smashed herself or sleeping. Would I have the audacity to walk into Papi's home if I was under the influence?

We soon reached Lisa's house. It is one of many multi-family homes on a semi-busy street. We enter through the back door to a first floor apartment. It is bright and clean but it looks like a library threw up inside. There is clutter everywhere! There are *"cachibaches"* (Peruvian terminology, go locate and then interrogate a Peruvian) in every corner. It is a kind of organized clutter but I am still shocked at the amount of crap they have. Making our way to the living room Lisa pushes a tower of books off the couch so we can sit. She plops herself on a love seat and sits on top of a pile of magazines.

I think she notices my shock because she admits, "Sydney never throws anything away she's a pack rat. Like Ricki Lake says, she is trying to compensate for something she was missing in her childhood. I try to clean up sometimes and throw stuff away but she notices. She goes into the garbage and brings the crap back in the house. I don't try anymore. Fuck it."

Nicki walks over to the small radio on the floor and puts on Hot 93.7. They are playing Rebirth of Slick by Digable Planets. She cranks it up and starts rapping along with the song. As we are all bobbing our heads, Nicki is putting on a show. She grabs an umbrella from the floor using it as a microphone.

"Just sendin chunky rhythms right down ya block

We be to rap what key be to lock"

As she is sliding across the "stage" Lisa comes back and starts dancing next to her. They finish their show and Yvette, Evelyn and I are trying to catch our breath from laughing so hard.

Breathing heavy, Lisa turns down the radio as she takes a long sip of an ice cold Heineken. Nicki sits on the loveseat and slides the end table in front of her. I take a seat on the floor opting for more room while Nicki grabs her book bag and retrieves a green baggie. She dumps it out on the table and begins breaking up the buds. More sooner than later I have to make up my mind if I am going to partake in the communal ganja. My mind still racing I smell the potent, familiar, aroma of the herb and it brings me back.

Marijuana has been used by ancient civilizations for recreational and medicinal use for ages. The Incas probably smoked weed and chewed on cocaine leaves and they were capable of creating a great and complex civilization atop massive mountains. Maybe it was even the reason why they were able to think outside the box and create such a mystifying place… because they were high.

"The Philly?" Nicki turns to Yvette.

"What Philly?" Yvette questions with a blank expression. "The Philly that you asked me to get the other day, the one we used on Wednesday?"

"Shit. Do you have one?" Nicki asks in desperation. Lisa shakes her head.

"Now don't look at me, you know I don't smoke the chronic. I'm keepin' my lungs the way I was born with them, clean." Evelyn says not looking up from a Home and Garden magazine she is flipping through.

Now this would be the point where I dig in my book bag and save the day and say, "I got one right here!" I can even picture the girls looking at me in admiration, but unfortunately I don't have one either.

"What the hell are we going to do? You know ain't nobody coming here just to bring us a Philly. If I call anybody they are going to want to smoke too and there already four of us smoking this tiny ass-nick." Nicki looks visibly upset. Feeling the desperation of having water with no cup, Nicki storms outside.

I smile and turn to Lisa, "Do you have an apple and tin foil?"

"Yeah, let's just bake a pie I'm hungry." Evelyn is rubbing her belly.

"Yes sir, I got apples. Grab one they're on top of the table." Lisa orders as she finishes her Heineken.

I go to the kitchen and grab an apple and find a sharp knife on the counter next to a roll of tin foil. I carry my items with me and set them on top of the little side table where Nicki left the weed. I sit down and begin carving into the apple from the top.

Lisa is scanning the stations for music when she stops at a commercial. The man's deep voice is advertising chicken on sale at C-Town in Spanish. He makes it sound so exciting! His captivating energy comes popping out of the speakers. This guy makes me want to go out and buy some chickens!

"*Ay Dios*. Change it please!" Yvette cries as she puts her hands to her ears.

Lisa smiles and ignores her. The DJ finishes the commercial and continues talking, dedicating the next song, "*Una mujercita extra-especial*." We hear Frankie Ruiz, "Desnudate Mujer" float through the airwaves. Shocked, Lisa quickly changes the station.

"Sorry, I just wanted Ady to hear who your Daddy was," she says apologizing.

"He knows Mami listens to his show all the time. Giving a shout out to your mistress while your wife is listening is just sick. I can't believe that man is my father," Yvette confesses looking disgusted.

"*Asi son los Dominicanos*," Evelyn mutters matter of factly.

"*Dominicanos nada*, Latino's in general are cheating buzzards but yeah, you right, *esos Dominicanos! Son los peores!*" Yvette mutters as she rolls her eyes, "Yeah you right. All my uncles, cousins, even my grandfather, the worst."

"He really that bad?" I question trying to form a mental picture of her father.

"Who, Yvette's father?" Nicki walks back in the house, still visibly irritated that we can't smoke. "He got cojones. I have an aunt who knows this woman whose cousin's roommate is a hairdresser who is messing around with him. He got no shame in his game." She continues as she walks over to me and my science experiment on the table. *Mr. Condon, I would have made you proud, minus the mandatory safety goggles!*

I am almost done constructing my masterpiece. I have smoked out of some strange things before: beer cans, watermelons, toilet paper rolls and yes, apples. I saw it made before but I was never the one making it. This is the first time that I was the creator of the "produce with potency." I am proud of my first attempt and hold it up, high, for the girls to see.

"Okay, who's ready to smoke, who got the lighter?" I ask, content that I saved the day. Looking around the room I notice the girls looking at me in amusement. No one says anything for a moment as they are faced with this new realm of smoking the bud.

"Girl, you are crazy. Are we really going to get high with that apple? I don't want to waste my nick if we are not going to get lit," Nicki says poetically.

I grab a red lighter and light the weed on top while inhaling deep through the hole on the side. Smart girls always think twice and I thought about it more than a few times. Was this something I definitely should not be doing? I decided the answer was, if I couldn't do it in front of Papi… I should not be doing it at all. As I take another toke I begin to get philosophical in my thinking as I tend to do when I get high. Maybe I was shifting from smoking to forget and escape my home life to just smoking to get to the lovely feeling when I get high. Now when I got high I would come down from that high to a safe and secure home life. But shit, I hope I came down before I got home because I don't know if I could have a conversation with Lorena if I was high. She also works with troubled teenage kids at the Salvation Army and I am pretty sure she knows what high looks like.

"Ady, you crazy! What are you going to do with that apple when you finish? Can I give it to my English teacher tomorrow? He's a jerk." Evelyn says with scorn.

"Who's your teacher?" I ask, thinking back to the incident with Mr. Casey.

"Mr. Casey. He really don't like me. I hate readin' but shit I try. In the beginning, I tried to do the homework but he was teachin' some complicated, off the wall shit. We were reading Romeo and Juliet and I just didn't know what the hell the book was about. I asked him for help once after class and asshole told me that he could only help so much. He told me I should hire a personal tutor!"

"I guess I'm not the only one." I say handing the apple to Nicki as I tell the girls about my ordeal with Mr. Casey earlier that day.

"All those teachers in that school are prejudice fuckers. I haven't had one yet that has gone out of their way to teach me a damn thing," Nicki says with a mouth full of smoke slowly exhaling with each word.

"Blah, blah, blah. How are you ever going to learn anything if you are always skipping school? What are they supposed to teach to, an empty seat? And when you do sit in class you got an attitude with the teachers anyways. How are they supposed to teach you if you always got that stink ass look on your face? It is what you make it." Lisa shrugs her shoulders, taking her turn and quickly passing the apple to Yvette.

"Let you tell it, white girl," Nicki says, laughing, "I wish we could trade places one day so you could see what gets thrown at me all the time and why I act the way I do. It's easy for you to blend in with the crowd and get treated with respect and have them think you gonna be somebody. I got this nappy hair to make me stick out and let them teachers know where I'm from. Now you tell me how you gonna make a cake out of a pile of shit."

Evelyn giggles, getting up to go the bathroom, "Ask Ady, she made a bowl out of an apple."

Yvette adds, "Even though we went to the same schools since we were little I don't think we were taught the same. You're expected to do good in your honors classes. They expect at least a passin' grade from me in mainstream. Remember in elementary, they thought I was slow because we speak Spanish in the house? They told Mami not to talk to me in both languages 'cause it would delay my learning. It took them this many years to realize I had dyslexia. If you keep telling a kid they stupid they going to start believing it after a while. And the other way around too, if I was constantly told since I was a kid that I was a genius, I bet you I would be sitting in those honor classes with you."

Evelyn came back with an armful of munchies she spread out on the coffee table.

I get comfortable and stretch out on the floor looking up at the ceiling. "So if we all looked like Lisa we'd all be in honors classes getting college credit right now?" I throw the question in the air, not directed at anyone in particular.

"I don't know if we would all be there but I think we would have a better opportunity at gettin' there." Yvette says slowly as if she is really thinking hard about the possibility.

We listen to 2pac's sweet voice singing "I Get Around" on the radio as we devour the rest of the junk food.

"But when you learn, you can't tie me down.

Baby doll, check it out, I get around."

I get up and get a glass of water from the kitchen. Maybe I can speed up the coming down from this high with some ice cold water in my system. I go back in the living room and sit on the floor as we chat and joke for what seems an eternity. Weed tends to freeze the clocks.

After a while Yvette looks at her watch and says, "I'm going to call Mami and see if she can pick me up before Daddy comes home. You need a ride?" she turns to me.

"Yeah, maybe I should be getting home."

"Your dad give you a curfew?" Evelyn inquires.

"He hasn't said nothing yet, I didn't ask. I don't think he would tell me when to come home as long as I don't get home too late," I reply, thinking about Papi and how he expects a lot from me. I think Papi is well aware that teenagers make bad choices and I feel like he will still be there after I fumble.

Evelyn confesses, "Mami doesn't want me home after 11 on the weekends. She said that *'una senorita'* should be in the house early and not out at all hours of the night. She knows damn well that I haven't been a senorita for years!

"My moms changes her mind about curfews, depends on her mood that day. If I get home early one day and roll through the door at 11 she yells at me and tells me I shoulda been home by 10. But most of the time I stay out till I get tired and want to go home. Don't give a damn what she says. I get home late, she complains, if I'm home, she complains. Either way, I get in trouble, so why not stay out and chill?" Nicki laughs.

"Well I got the party house, so I'm always home. I don't have problems with Sydney about getting home late. Even if I did, she doesn't notice when I'm home anyways. As long as I wash my own dishes she doesn't care," Lisa said as she grabs the ashtray and lights her cigarette.

"Okay. Mami *viene ahora*. Let's go outside so I can smoke a cigarette before she gets here." Yvette motions to me. I get up and grab my book bag, snatch the magic apple from the table, and join the girls on the front porch.

It is still light out and the sun is beaming bright. Yvette and Lisa are smoking on one side of the porch while Evelyn and Nicki are covering their mouths with their shirts on the other side of the porch, swatting away the smoke. I take a seat on the steps, right in the middle. I dismantle the black and red apple, breaking it into little pieces.

"What are you doing?" Lisa says, waving her pack of cigarettes at me to see if I want one.

I shake my head. "Na, I'm good. You can't throw this in the garbage. What if your mom sees it while she's looking for something you threw away?" I begin to throw little pieces of blackened apple over the side of the porch into the bushes. "It's biodegradable; it'll just rot in da ground."

Laughing, Evelyn jumps off the porch, "Well ladies. I'm out. See yall Monday. I'm going to New York this weekend to see Santo. And don't even say anything Lisa, you do it too, but just on the down low. I have no shame in loving more than one dude. Peace yall." She blows a kiss in the air, smiles and spins around to cross the street. She is a peppy Puerto Rican if I ever did see one. She is not one to sugar coat the truth.

A little red Toyota pulls into the driveway. Taking one last, long, drag of her cigarette Yvette jumps up, "See you next Tuesday!"

"Bye! Hope we can chill again soon, this was relaxing." I tell the girls.

As I run to the car, I faintly hear Nicki shout out after me. "Check you later, MacGyver!"

Chaos Theory

FADE TO BLACK... SIX MONTHS LATER

Another day, another bother. It had been raining all night and the sun is now trying to break through the clouds. I climb out of the security of my warm bed, stretch, and get up to start my day. I look around my room for my *pantuflas, chancletas* (for you Puerto Ricans), and slippers (for the rest). Yes, *my* room. We made the big move from New Britain to West Hartford during the summer vacation. We moved into a newly constructed house on South Quaker Lane in a cute little complex called Spice Glen. I was excited to make the move into the freshly painted house on the fragrant street called Ginger Lane. The lack of a backyard is a small price to pay for the three level house and quiet neighborhood. A small price to me anyway, oblivious to the fact that the price tag on the house would leave a huge dent every month on Papi's paycheck.

Papi quietly constructed the crib and placed it right in front of their bed in the Master bedroom, as if maybe if he was quiet enough, I wouldn't notice my baby sister was in there. When I first moved in with Papi, Lorena was already three months pregnant. They didn't tell me when they found out at first because they didn't want to upset me (or so they said). They thought that news of a new baby would anger me in some way, so they kept it a secret for months.

So there I was, in a brand new house, with the blessing of a new baby sister, in a safe neighborhood, attending a top ranked high school, taking a nice hot shower waiting to go downstairs to eat a hearty breakfast. With all my cards nicely laid out in my favor I should have been settled down, happy, taking advantage of the cards laid out before me. But despite all my good fortune, I am still getting in trouble at school, not studying, and still drinking and smoking.

I turn on the radio and change the stations until I heard the familiar lyrics of Gang Starr.

"Check your nearest overpopulated ghetto

They greet you with a pistol not

Trying to say hello"

I love music but I have never been one to sing along with a song or dance around the room. Singing in the shower or dancing around naked was never my thing even though I am a music fanatic. Sadly, I was born without any rhythm, debunking the myth that all Latinos know how to dance.

Slipping on my size 4 black and tan Reeboks, I follow the smell of bacon downstairs. I give Lorena a kiss on the cheek, "Morning."

"*Buenos dias, Beba. ¿Que tal dormiste?*" she asks. I grew up with that phrase. "Good morning… how did you sleep?" Maybe that predates to the olden days when mattresses were made of straw and sleep was horrible. I grab a fried yucca off the plate next to the stove and go into the fridge to grab some O.J. The fridge is filled to capacity and there is a big pot of something marinating.

"I slept fine. What's for dinner?" I'm curious what gourmet meal I have waiting for me when I get home.

She sticks out her tongue, "*Lengua,*" she replies with a grin, knowing it is not my favorite dish. One would think that cow tongue is the most disgusting thing you can ever eat but leave it in Lorena's hands and it turns into a mouthwatering stew. She cooks it for hours in a bath of spices, peas and carrots and it magically turns into something edible. Not my favorite, but safe to eat.

Lorena places a plate full of scrambled eggs, fried yucca, and bacon in front of me. Luckily, I haven't gained a pound since I moved in with Papi. I am still a size one despite my aversion to anything remotely athletic.

Wolfing down my delectable breakfast I begin the day on a positive note, with a full stomach. All the studies about the difficulty of learning on an empty stomach only factored in people who *wanted* to learn. I would be the anomaly in the experiment; I have a full stomach with no desire to learn. Why should I go out of my way pushing and shoving to get ahead of all these students who were groomed to take full advantage of their education? How easy would it be to sit in a classroom with a teacher who has been a friend of the family for years, with a teacher that looked like you? I start giggling at the image of Mr. Casey coming to dinner tonight to dine on cow tongue.

"What are you laughing at, *loca*?" Lorena asks, laughing herself.

"Nothing, just daydreaming. Is the baby awake yet?" Eager to play with her before I leave for school.

"*Sube, esta en la cama con tu Papa,*" she points upstairs with the spatula.

I run up to Papi's room and crack the door to see if they are awake. Papi is in bed with Bianca propped up on his belly. He is smiling at her and reciting a nursery rhyme to her in Spanish. "*Pin pon es un muñeco con cara de cartón... se lava la carita... con agua y con jabón...*" Papi was always the one to keep us close to our traditions. It is due to him that I didn't totally lose my knowledge of Spanish. When Mami and Papi arrived here, it was Mami who spoke to us only in English and eventually stopped speaking Spanish altogether. She told Papi that since we were in the United States he needed to speak the language. Papi thought the opposite, since English would be our primary language while in the United States, he should try and preserve our Spanish. Luckily, growing up Papi kept speaking to us exclusively in Spanish and we replied back in Spanish. He actually told us that he didn't know English. One day Mami, tired of Papi's little white lie, told me that Papi knew English very well. Until the age of six I thought that Papi didn't know a word of English, although he was very fluent.

"Hi Papi, good morning." I give him a kiss and climb in the bed to play with my new sister. She is tiny and fat at the same time, a little sumo wrestler in pink frilly PJ's. Her skin is snow white and her already long, pointy hair is dark black. She looks at me with dark, wide eyes and stares at me as if I interrupted something very important.

"*¿Dormiste bien? Bianca estaba llorando anoche.*" He said apologizing for Bianca's late night wails.

"I slept fine, I didn't hear her. But I gotta run. I don't want to miss my ride," I glance at the clock on the wall. It is a finely detailed mirror clock made in Peru. It matches the rest of the decorations in the house, Peruvian high end décor. I wonder if any of my teachers have llamas or ritual sacrificial knives adorning their walls at home.

"*¿Te llevo?*" Papi offers a ride, even though I have been getting rides from a friend to school since the start of the school year.

"No, that's okay. Stay with the little Monchichi." I say running my hands through her soft hair. I jump out of the bed and gave them both quick kisses. "Love you!"

I reach my friend's house in less than two minutes; he lives five houses down from me. Jeremy is a few years older than me, a quiet Puerto Rican from a "good family". There is no single mom or father in jail or sisters living on welfare type stories in his family. The only smudge on his image is the fact that he became a father when he was in middle school. Anyways, he offered to bring me to school in the mornings when he found out I moved right down the street.

"Good morning!" I say as I jump into his tiny little black Mazda. His cousin Jessi is already in the front seat.

"Hey," they both ring out in unison.

"What's good little one, you hungry? We 'bout to go to McDonalds on Kane Street to get some grub. Strait?" Jeremy said, never one to stress over getting to school on time.

"I'm full but that's fine." I say glancing at the dashboard at the clock. Another detention for being late. One more and I would win a Saturday detention! Four hours on an early Saturday morning of complete silence and pure boredom. The thrill of the day would be when Mr. Brown would lift his arm to write the amount of time left till we were released, revealing his incredibly huge, gross ring of sweat invading his armpit.

"Did you hear about that *Americano* from school that committed suicide yesterday?" Jessi whispers as if she doesn't want to announce it to the world.

"I didn't hear nothing. Why, what happened?" I'm curious, I never wake up early enough to watch the morning news.

Jeremy replies, "Yeah, Jacob! I went to elementary school with him. Cool kid. I wasn't friends with him, he was younger than me but we knew each other. Happened last night, he went outside and hung himself with a *hamaca* in the backyard. They didn't find him 'till early this morning. His mom went crazy when she found him, they had to admit her to the hospital."

"Wow, that's some off the wall shit. I can't imagine anything would ever make me want to end it all." I say in shock about the situation. I don't know the kid, never met him, but I do have compassion for the family he left behind. I see it more through the eyes of the mother and father who now have to outlive their son. To me, suicide is a selfish act that ultimately involves more than just the individual who is suffering.

"This is like the third student I know who has committed suicide since middle school. It's sad that these kids are killing themselves. I don't get it," he says pausing to order at the window. "It don't make no sense at all."

"I bet you a *platano* all three were *Americanos*, right?" Jessi asks, already formulating an answer in her head.

"You ever heard about a Puerto Rican committing suicide? Or *un cocolo* from the projects found hung in his room? Call me up when you see that on the 6:00 news." Jeremy replies, as we wait in the drive thru lane.

"*Imaginate*! Trying to survive a day in the projects. Drive bys, crack heads, overdoses, stick ups, just to make it to your room and end it yourself. Now *that* don't make no sense," Jessi remarks, grabbing her food.

"Maybe if we dropped that kid off in Charter Oak on D side for a few days he would still be alive." I say visualizing a skinny pale kid walking through the local projects, Charter Oak Terrace, on a hot summer day. Scared and confused, maybe his problems would be put into perspective and he would see that his life was not that unbearable. But on the other hand, I never felt such desperation so I can't assume anything. From the inside, maybe his big house and perfect family was not so perfect. Maybe the ugly truth, that only he knew, led him to end his life.

"Mami told me if I ever committed suicide she would come to the other side and open up a can of whoop -ass," Jeremy jokes.

We drive the rest of the way to school with the radio blasting Mr. Wendal by Arrested Development.

"Uncivilized we call him,

but I just saw him eat off the food we waste

Civilization, are we really civilized, yes or no?

Who are we to judge?"

I go to the main office to sign myself in with an unexcused tardy again. I forge notes from my father sometimes saying that I have doctors' appointments but you can only do that so many times before they think that you are dying of a terminal illness. So I sign in and wait for the secretary to hand me over the Saturday detention sentence. Looking out of sorts, she hands me a pass and tells me to report to my homeroom instead of my first period.

"The principal has an important announcement to make so hurry sweetie." she says in a shaky voice. I look up at her and I notice her red puffy eyes. I didn't realize that this morning she woke up to sirens and two ambulances pulling up to her neighbor's house. One ambulance took a son who was already gone and the other was for the mom who was panic-stricken and in hysterics. The secretary and Jacob's mom had been best friends for years.

I grab the pass and head quickly to my homeroom. By now the word has already gotten around about Jacob. There were students crying quietly with wads of tissues in their hands. As I take a seat at my desk the principal's voice booms over the loudspeaker. Yvette glances over at me from the next seat and flashes me a tight squeeze of the eyes and a crinkled nose.

"Folks, I have an important announcement to make that will affect the whole student body here at Conard High School. I am very sad to say that there has been an untimely death here at Conard. Jacob Wakefield, a freshman here, was found early this morning at his home. His family will be holding a memorial service this Sunday at Saint Bridget church on New Britain Avenue at 1:00. For those of us who knew Jacob I understand that this will be a difficult time for us. The district has provided us with onsite counselors that will be available to students this week in the library. If you feel that you need to talk to someone just notify your teacher and they will give you a pass to see a grief counselor. We will also be having a candlelight vigil tonight for friends and family in the side courtyard at 7:00 P.M. I would also like to take this time to let each one of you know that if you are having a difficult time in your life please let someone know. We are here to help, we are a family here at Conard and we are here for each other. Remember, my door is always open."

The loudspeaker crackles and then goes dead. The room is quiet for a few minutes as we all looked to the homeroom teacher for cues about what to do next. I hear someone sniffling in the back row. One student grabs his things and leaves the room without a word. The air is filled with sadness and confusion about what to do next. I never knew anybody who committed suicide. Jeremy said that this was the third kid he knew who did this. How can such a huge tragedy happen so often in one community? Was it something in the water? My thoughts are cut short by the teachers attempt to unify the classroom.

"Okay you guys, I guess we are here until the bell rings. Does anyone have any questions or concerns about what the principal spoke about?" The teacher asks her questions nervously. Mrs. Smith is a fairly young teacher and she looks very uncomfortable talking about the tragedy. She looks horrified when the classroom stays silent.

"Okay, well I just think that some kind of dialogue would be healthy in a situation like this. Umm. Well, sometimes when teenagers are transitioning from childhood into adolescence they find it awkward and have feelings of being alone…" Mrs. Smith rambles on for a while and starts to sound like the teacher in Peanuts. *WHAH WHAH WHAH WHAH WHAH WHAH…*

Yvette throws me a wadded up piece of paper. I catch it with one hand and read the note: 'This is whack. When Edwin died they didn't even mention it at school.' Edwin lived with his mom in a Latin King infested street on the border of West Hartford and Hartford. Edwin's mom, scared for her son's life and future, was ready to move out of the neighborhood. With a content heart and a prosperous future ahead of them Edwin told his mom he was going to say his goodbyes to his friends in the neighborhood the day they were moving. Within an hour, a car full of *Solidos* pulled up to Edwin and his two friends while they were walking. They shot both his friends in the knees, turned to Edwin, and shot him in the back of the head.

The girls recall during the funeral people throwing yellow and black rosaries into his coffin. His mother went ballistic! She grabbed a bunch of them and threw them at random people screaming, "This is your fault! It's your fault I don't have my baby! He was no gangbanger!" Crying hysterically she had collapsed on the floor in front of Edwin's coffin.

Noticing the flying note, Mrs. Smith stops her rambling short, "Yvette, Ady, do you ladies have anything to add?" Looking at each other we both shake our heads.

Of all the stories the girls told me about Edwin they always talked about him being totally against gang life. He was a kind, sweet, caring son that didn't want to break his mother's heart by losing another son to gang violence. He never claimed loyalty to anyone.

The bell rings and we all gathered our things and scurry out like roaches. Reaching Yvette's locker we meet up with the girls. The normalcy of the day is disrupted and it feels like a Friday afternoon instead of a Monday morning. We see crowds of people walking off school grounds and people gathering in the courtyard. It seems like class is an option today and the administration doesn't have enough manpower to keep the students from creating an uncontrollable chaos.

"I'm about to be out, anybody want to roll?" Nicki asks the group looking unfazed about the whole situation.

"Where you going?" Yvette questions.

"Boobie's coming to pick me up in a few." Boobie got his unfortunate nickname from his childhood obesity and the unsightly womanly breasts he possessed. He is a few years older than us and goes to a technical high school in Hartford. He lives in the Charter Oak Terrace projects with his mom and he is a sweetheart. Even though he roughed up a few people here and there and was a willing participant to a few drive bys, he was a kind person. That is exactly the reason that he and Nicki are only friends. She told me that he was too nice to date, even though he is madly in love with her.

"I'm going home. I had enough drama for one day. I just want to go home and sleep." Lisa replies, waving to us with a gloomy frown.

"Wait I'll walk home with you!" Evelyn calls out to Lisa, "Y'all stupid. I moved to Connecticut to get out of the projects!" she says as she runs to catch up with Lisa.

"Strait, I'll go," I reply, not wanting to sit in an empty classroom.

"I don't want to be in class right now," Yvette says, looking around the crowded hallway.

We stuff our book bags in my locker and spill out into the student parking lot. The usually barren parking lot is alive with people standing around talking and jumping in their cars and leaving. We are hardly noticed as we walk to the main road to meet Boobie. He pulls up driving a beat up blue Toyota. His cars are always old and falling apart but I never see him in the same car twice. Had I known that some of them were stolen, I would have thought twice about getting into the car.

"Ladies! ¿*Como estan?*" he says with a grand smile. Having lost most of his childhood poundage Boobie is a handsome Puerto Rican. He is still a big boy but he is far from unsightly. His complexion is pale in the winter and bronze in the summer.

Nicki walks over to the passenger seat and opens the door staring down Boobie's friend until he reluctantly gets out and resigns himself to the backseat with me and Yvette. Boobies' friend Tone is very short both in stature and personality. Not very bright and super immature he is kind of like an empty paper bag sitting next to Boobie. Tone gives us a quick hello and turns his attention back to the 40 ounce festively wrapped in a brown paper bag that he is nursing first thing in the morning.

"Ady what's good? How's your pops?" Boobie asks as he looks at me in the cracked rear view mirror.

"He's good, working hard like always. Why you not in class right now? We have an excuse, you should be in school." Wondering why he is picking us up on a Monday, instead of being in class. Boobie has the potential for success in the future if he makes the right choices and stays clear of drama and stray bullets.

"We got shop this week, finished classes last week," Boobie replies, driving towards Hartford, "I did my part already I'm just waiting on my partner. I'm graduating next year for sure, you'll see. I gotta take care of Mami, she be working too much."

"You're too good Boobie. I'm not giving my mom shit when I get a job," Nicki frowns as she rolls down the window, "She'll probably ask me for back rent from when I was a baby."

"I hear you Boobie. Papi won't have to work anymore when I get my job. That's the least I can do," I say, despite not having a clear plan for the future. Somehow I am going to graduate high school and college and get a career in something that will make enough money to provide for me, Mami, Papi and my grandmother in Peru. Graduating from high school was never a question in my mind. Going to college and getting my degree? That is a must. That is why Mami and Papi moved to the United States; so we would be able to take advantage of the opportunities provided here. Although I was raised knowing this and what was expected of me… I was still on my way to the projects in a stolen car on a Monday morning instead of sitting in a classroom.

"Can we stop by the corner store? I am starving and Ady's stomach is growling." Yvette throws out while poking me in the stomach.

We reach the beginning of Park Street and are immediately hit with the appetizing aroma of *"pura comida Latina"*. A symphony of smells flows through the car windows: *cubanitos* from Boriquen Bakery, *mondongo* from El Comerio, and burritos from El Mercado. It is really too much for me to handle. My stomach roars and demands to be fed. Driving down Park Street is like boarding a plane and getting off in the middle of San Juan. The mostly Puerto Rican owned businesses and churches are infused with just a pinch of other Latin American flavor. The noise and trash filled streets are reminiscent of a neighborhood carnival. As we pull up to the tiny corner store we pile out of the car while Boobie double parks.

"*Mira* Boobie! *Cuando vas a venir a comer a mi casa!*" A young, tired looking girl screams out the second floor window on top of the corner store. Hair in rollers, she is practically falling out the window as she ashes her cigarette, cinders falling over our heads as we walk in the store. Nicki looks back at Boobie like she is going to kill him later. He doesn't react to the girl as he shrugs his shoulders and smiles sweetly at Nicki, turning his attention to a car full of guys. They pulled up in a new car with tints and rims with the music blaring.

"*Dame tres Cubanitos*, please," Yvette said to the store clerk trying to dodge his improper stares. As we pool our money together I hand over my two dollars, more than enough to cover the enormous dollar sandwich that I will devour in one minute flat. Nicki asks the clerk for two Phillies and Yvette grabs her pack of Newport lights. Waiting for the sandwiches to be made Nicki peers out the window.

"That's Juacho and them dudes talking to Boobie," Nicki says, straining her eyes while peering out of the dirty, grimy store window to see outside.

"Those guys that use to roll with your father?" I ask remembering Nicki mentioning them coming around once in a while to check up on her. Juacho and her father were best friends and he promised Nicki's father he would always keep an eye out for her "when" he got murdered. Yes, "when" he got murdered. Nicki's father always knew that he would never grow old. Nicki's father was a far cry from my own dad.

"Let's stay in here for a little bit till they leave. I don't feel like talkin' to him right now." Nicki says picking up an old dusty *Vanidades* magazine from the rack. A few minutes pass and they peel away, leaving tire marks on the pothole infested road.

"Let's go, I'm starvin!" I say grabbing our grocery bag of goodies. The clerk stares us down and says something undecipherable in his heavy Dominican twang.

"*Viejo sucio.*" Yvette calls back at him as we walk out the door.

"Hey where's my samich?" Boobie questions looking at each one of us. "Ya'll didn't get me one?"

"Hum. I thought you was going to go eat at your girl's house that's why I didn't get you one." Nicki says lifting her chin towards the girl hanging out the window. Nicki didn't want anything to do with Boobie but at the same time she didn't like seeing him with alternate options.

"Her mom is friends with Mami, trying to make it sound like I chill with her. You know my heart belongs to my queen." He kisses Nicki's hand and snatches half of the sandwich that she is holding. "Oh and speaking of Queens, your boy Juacho was grillin me about you. He heard you was going to be initiated. What is he talking 'bout?" Boobie quickly stops the car for a runaway Piragua cart that jumps into traffic with its owner quickly following.

"People trying to get me to, but I don't know about that. I'm not having a group of girls beat me down while I just sit there without swinging. That just aint me. Just 'cause my pops was a King don't mean shit," she says while she bites her fingernails.

"You know that's some silly shit, you smarter than that Nicki." Boobie says bracing himself for the response he knows he is going to get.

"I will do what I damn well please. I don't need you tellin' me what is good for me, I do as I choose and I don't need your permission. That's my decision to make on my own. I don't need your corny ass opinion!" Nicki yells harshly to Boobie.

The normally quiet Tone speaks and says a little louder than a whisper, "Boobie you a punk ass letting a chick talk to you like that." As soon as the comment crosses his lips I know by his expression that he wants to take it back. Like slow motion, I see Nicki quickly spin around in her seat and punch Tone square in the face with her right fist then with her left she grabs his beer and tosses it out the window. Shocked, I scoot towards Yvette narrowly missing Nicki's fists of fury. Practically sitting on top of Yvette I let out a nervous giggle. Nicki is no joke; I'm glad she is on my side.

Stopping the car in mid-traffic Boobie screams out, "Nicki what the fuck?!"

Nicki jumps out of the passenger's seat into oncoming traffic and screams, "You want to keep running your mouth Tone? I'm not sitting in the car with this asshole."

"Don't worry Nicki, I'm out. You lucky I don't hit girls. I'm out." Tone screeches, despite the fact that we all knew he beat his girlfriend on a daily basis. He has a line of blood dripping down his cheek from the blow by Nicki's knuckle ring. As he climbs out of the car he turns to Boobie, "Boo you don't need someone like that in ya life."

Nicki gets back in the car as we all sit in silence. I climb off the security of Yvette's lap and plop over to the other side of the car. The adrenaline is still pumping and we all need a few minutes to process the craziness that just exploded in the car. Yvette glances at me with a frown of disappointment and shrugs her shoulders. Staring out the window I watch the rows and rows of abandoned buildings that clutter the Hartford skyline. Graffiti decorates the buildings with scenes of guns, crowns, and profiles with tear drops. Artists' names are immortalized by the graffiti on the wall. I think about the people who lived in these beautiful homes a hundred years ago. Did they ever imagine that their neighborhood would turn into this wasteland? Hartford looks like a Dali painting, melting clocks, crazy images, and a sad undertone. A huge tag of a colorful butterfly adorns the entryway of an abandoned Victorian home.

"Do you know that the flap of a butterfly's wings can affect the weather thousands of miles away?" I say absentmindedly. *Ooops that just slipped out, I didn't mean to say that out loud.* I was watching the Discovery Channel with Papi last night, one of the many pastimes we enjoy together and they were analyzing Chaos Theory. I tried very hard to picture Nicki doing the same, sitting with her father watching documentaries. Maybe the instability in her life caused her to be the way she is. She is constantly demanding respect from everyone through a cloud of insecurity.

Looking back at me, Nicki says, "What the hell does that have to do with anything? You be thinking 'bout some silly shit, Ady." Everyone chuckles and the hostility in the air seems to dissipate.

Not wanting to get into the technical aspects of the Butterfly Effect I ponder the theory. Tiny variations can affect giant systems. Was I defining my future by surrounding myself with violence, drugs, and negativity? Little did I know that I would be able to change those choices in the near future, find my wings and ultimately change my own destiny.

"Do you know... that if you punch someone in the face in Hartford... someone sneezes in China?" Nicki says slowly. The car bursts into laughter as we drive into the local projects: Charter Oak Terrace.

****

Here the little boy grew up in poverty and dealt with misfortune that made him into the man that I would eventually marry.

Pegao

Charter Oak Terrace is located off of Flatbush Avenue in Hartford where it seems dark clouds permanently cover the 1,000 units of public housing. The worn down, sad looking complexes are in desperate need of repair or a wrecking ball. The lack of trees and grass make it feel like a concrete stage with a cast of clowns and puppets, and the only green you see in the streets is in the exchange of money from drug transactions. The grounds are alive with constant activity, there are people bursting out of the seams. People are decorating their front stoops, in the street, sitting on top of their cars, or hanging out their second story windows. The air is alive with the chatter and commotion of the everyday lives of the people who call Charter Oak home sweet home.

Boobie turns into one of the parking lots and pulls up next to a discarded mattress covered in stains. "I gotta stop by Maria's house for a second. She locked up in dat house don't even go out to get her mail no more." As he jumps out of the car, a gang of rats scurry for safety under a nearby dumpster.

"Who's Maria?" I turn to Nicki, curious why this lady doesn't leave her house, assuming she is a little old lady who can't move around too well.

"Remember that murder the day before New Year's? They found that father and son dead and then they found the son's best friend dead too, a few blocks away. Marvin was Maria's son. She lost her husband, son and her adopted son all in the same day. They would all still be here if Marvin didn't mess with that cane. He tried selling it then he got curious and ended up using all his supply! He tried to hide but they found him, tortured, then killed em. Killed the father and the best friend just for fun I guess, to fuck with his head before they got to Marvin. Maria was in Puerto Rico, that's the only reason she still alive. People gossiping, saying she was with her other man over there and now she feels mad guilty." The story comes out of her mouth like she is telling a child a bedtime story. No sadness, no shock, as if this is a norm for her chaotic life.

I imagine a triple homicide scene in the clean and pristine streets of my neighborhood of Spice Glen, located not even two miles down the street from Charter Oak. This was not supposed to be the destiny for a "temporary" housing complex that was built during World War II to shelter defense workers. The early days of community involvement and nicely groomed lawns of Charter Oak Terrace were short lived. The Hartford Housing Authority tried in the beginning to maintain a policy of controlled integration limiting the number of black families that could move in but eventually the shift was made. As black families moved in, white families that occupied Charter Oak Terrace hastily packed up their shit and moved to the suburbs. Then the tobacco industry in Connecticut during the 80's attracted many Puerto Ricans who quickly populated the affordable housing in Charter Oak Terrace. *Vaya, there goes the neighborhood!!!*

Over the years, the area took an ugly turn for the worse. A permanent eyesore seen from I-84 for people commuting from New York to Boston, Charter Oak Terrace and its ugly twin, Rice Heights, are the unofficial symbol of Hartford and its lack of prosperity.

"I saw that in the paper," Yvette said, "They didn't know who the hell did it. Something about heavy drug dealing in the area where the bodies were found but that it didn't seem to be gang-related. What does one have to do with the other? Like they didn't know what to blame it on so if you put drugs and gang related in the same sentence with Charter Oak it makes it okay. *Que vaina!* Nobody will question it. Maybe it was a robbery, why don't they ever blame it on a burglary?" Yvette questions as she closes her window to block the stench of garbage that is seeping in from the dumpster.

"You know damn well they didn't have no valuables in the house," Nicki says sarcastically, "What are they going to steal? The silverware? The cash in the safe behind the Picasso?"

"No, but why they assume that just because they lived in Charter Oak that it was definitely not a burglary? Plenty of drug dealers with plenty of stuff to steal live here." Yvette points in emphasis to a shiny, Cadillac that has pulled up to the complex in front of us, a young kid stepping out of it and pulling a paper grocery bag out from the trunk.

"That shit makes no sense to me right there." I say as I spit my gum out the window. "Why you spend like forty thousand on a car and still be living here in the projects? Why not put a down payment on a nice house with that money?"

"Maybe, 'cause when you buy a car in cash no one asks questions but you can't buy a whole house in cash unless you're really flossin'," Nicki pronounces, "I don't think you can put down on a home loan application that your occupation is a drug dealer. We don't get weekly paychecks. You put unemployed, they won't give you a dime, even if you can pay your mortgage every month in cash. That's why they still live here."

Never being exposed to the trials and tribulations of a drug dealer, I take Nicki's word for it. The only drug dealer I know is Nicki, and she is just getting into the trade. She finally discovered a way to make money to pay her mother for the rent that she so desperately demanded. She would become a drug dealer. There is no age requirement, she doesn't have to wear a silly uniform, she doesn't get taxed on it, and she is an expert in the merchandise she is selling. She wasn't making much but she was able to give her mom money every month. Her mother never once asked her where the cash was coming from.

As Boobie walks back to the car we hear yells coming from every other stoop, "Hey Boobie! What's good! Yo! *Mira, muchacho!*" He stops and gives a kiss to an elderly lady who is sitting on her front lawn in a dilapidated plastic lawn chair with an infant on her lap. He jumps in the car with a heavy sigh.

"I think it's nice you know everyone in the neighborhood and they so friendly with you and your fam. I don't know anyone on my street," I think about the clear sense of community there is here even with the obvious "lack of's" they possess.

"You know why there is never anyone outside where you live at?" Boobie says, peeling out of the driveway. "Because they got 9 to 5's and then they get home and they tired, that's why. Here, don't hardly nobody have a job, so they sit outside all day and then they sit outside s'more."

"Don't your Mom got a 9 to 5?" Nicki pipes up, trying to start another debate where only she could win.

"I'm not sayin' that *nobody* in Charter Oak works Nicki. I am just sayin' that *most* people that live here are on State and don't got a job. Would you go out and get a job if your rent is being paid every month by Section 8? Man, as soon as you catch some income, even if it's minimum wage they take it away from you. *'Chacha*, what would you choose? Watchin' novellas and chillin' all day to pay the bills or workin' at McDonalds all day to pay da bills?" He puts up one hand and then the other like a scale.

"I wish my parents had that choice, they always had to bust their ass," Yvette replies with a laugh, "When they came to the U.S. they couldn't collect from the State. Ya'll *Portoros* are mad spoiled!"

I thought about my own situation and how my parents came to the U.S so that they could *work hard* and make sure that we would have opportunities to work hard and excel in life. Even after I was born here and they gained American citizenship they never looked to get any kind of assistance as we made ends meet. I grew up with the philosophy that there were always people worse off than us and all we had to do was look back to Peru for plenty of examples. A third world country with real world poverty. Papi always thought that receiving welfare assistance would just be taking much needed assistance from someone else down the line that needed it more than us. We were able bodied people that had the capacity to work for what we needed.

"Spoiled ain't the word; it's more like rotten, like we got the short end of the stick. The government *wants* us to sit and rot in our homes and not go out there and try and better ourselves. Keep us at home on welfare, pay our bills and we won't go out and get educated. *Verda'*. An educated nigga is more dangerous than a nigga with a burner. Of course we gonna choose to stay home and get our bills paid if you gonna throw it in our faces! That's the way they make sure that we ain't gonna start thinking for ourselves. Check this, military niggas be laughin' at us every time someone say they on Section 8. Look up what Section 8 means in military terms and tell me that the government didn't do that shit on purpose." Boobie preaches, revealing part of the conspiracy theory that he always swears by.

"You been watchin' Malcolm X again?!" Nicki overenthusiastically replies to Boobie's observations.

"Well, you gotta break the chain," I reply. "That's why you gotta stop messin' around and get that college degree. Let that diploma be your gun instead of the one you hide under ya bed." He kept a mini sawed off shotgun under his bed, *'Por se acaso'*.

"Yeah Boobie, pull yourself up from your bootstraps and all that good shit." Nicki adds, looking back at me with a smirk. "You can do it! Get out da projects, go to college and get a good job and make ya mama proud. But wait..." she says glancing back at me, "How's he gonna pull himself up by his bootstraps, when he aint got no shoes? You gotta be realistic Ady, Boobie got too many strikes against him to be anything but what he was born into."

Yvette turns to me, waiting for a reasonable reply with her eyebrows raised. Shit, but Nicki did make a valid point. I am not a male Puerto Rican living in the projects. My optimism is coming from my side of the fence, not from his reality.

"*Mujeres*, thank you for plannin' out my future," Boobie says with a shake of his head, "*Mucha' gracia'*, let me know what you decide. Let's get some grub."

"Straight, I'm starving!" I blurt out, even as the large sandwich I just ate is still digesting.

We all pile in Boobie's stuffy cramped two bedroom tenement. The cracked, water stained walls are adorned with religious paintings. Jesus' sad eyes are eerily following me around the tiny living room. I was raised as an Optional-Roman-Catholic where church was an option reserved for only special occasions like Easter, Christmas and times when we were down on our luck. I don't really know what I believe in. I like the idea of worshiping *Pachamama* (no not the black lady on your syrup bottle) and Inti, tangible things, more than the idea of an almighty God that I can't see. I feel the sun and the earth everyday so I have more of a connection with them than the son of God. I also hold some suspicion for a religion that was violently shoved down my ancestors' throats.

I look around the cluttered shelves filled with dusty, yellowing capias (you know, those cheesy little party favors that you get only when you go to a Latino fiesta?) collected from baby showers and weddings from the last twenty years. A shelf filled with happy hopes and new feelings of prosperity that sadly over the years have probably transformed into divorce and incarceration. Are Julio and Marisol still happily married after 15 years (maybe, if she hasn't found out yet about Lilly)? Do the little baby booties that decorated Luis Falcon's capia run through his memory as he sits in jail for 10 to life (maybe he reminisces about it with his new lifelong boyfriend)?

"Damn, Boobie it's hot as fuck in here!" Nicki calls out as she steps into the kitchen.

Boobie cracks the backdoor in the kitchen that peers out into the central courtyard. There are kids and teenagers hanging outside despite the fact that it is a school day. "There's food on the stove, *sirvencen.*"

I look over to the stove and see the usual menu; *chuletas, tostones* and *arroz con gandules. Delicious!* This is not the regular menu for me at home. I grab a Styrofoam plate from the counter and serve myself from a mountain of food. There is no shortage of food here. I am always amazed at the size of Puerto Rican rice pots, sitting on two burners; it looks like it is going to fall off the stove. Stomach growling, I take a seat at the wobbly plastic table next to the open door. Boobie grabs a huge trash bag from the floor and exposes a family of roaches that are also partaking in a lunch fest. *Gross!* I was not graced with the presence of roaches in the houses that I grew up in. They were never a part of my extended family.

"Ady, *pegao*?" Nicki offers, holding up a spoonful of, what seems to me, burnt rice.

"Na, I'm good, that don't look edible Nicki." I say not in tune with the delicacy of *pegao* and its apparent deliciousness. I think the dinner of cow tongue that is waiting for me at home would create the same reaction for Nicki. It's an acquired taste, like Malta. *Nastiness in a bottle.*

Nicki fills her plate and takes a seat next to me, grabbing the ketchup from the fridge, drowning her plate in it. She also eats Doritos dipped in ketchup on the regular.

I get up and turn on the tiny radio on top of the fridge. Ahmad's "Back in The Day" crackles over the busted speakers. We sit at the kitchen table listening to the radio while stuffing our faces, the sunlight beams shining on the cracked linoleum floor. Children are laughing outside, mothers are screaming at the top of their lungs for them to quiet down. The familiarity and comfort of Boobie's world is not my own. I am just a quiet and brief visitor in what he calls his permanent life.

Foreseeing my future, Ahmad's lyrics spill out,

"I miss those days, and so I pout like a grown jerk.

Wishin' all I had to do now, was finish homework.

It's true you don't realize really what you got 'til it's gone... back in the days."

"Damn," Yvette says with a glance at her watch as she gets up from the table, "I gotta get back to school before the last bell."

After rushing to get back, we make it a few minutes after the last bell of the day rings. As I push myself against the crowd I am reminded of the tragedy that sparked our field trip as people walk by sobbing. Saying my goodbyes to the girls I make my way to my locker and grab a few books, just for show, like accessories. I run to the student parking lot to catch my ride with Jeremy.

Exhausted, we make our way home with the radio blasting. Reaching my quiet road, we pull up to my home, disrupting the tranquility on my clean and orderly street. As I close the front door, I leave the drama of suicides, triple homicides, stolen cars, sucker punches, gang wars, and drug dealing on the welcome mat.

"¿Porque preguntas?"

FADE TO BLACK- FAST FORWARD - TWO YEARS LATER

I sit on the bed as she packs her suitcase; she is going back to Peru to get the divorce papers signed. She says she will be back before I know it, but I am still sad to see her go. She stuffs her suitcase to capacity with old clothes that she will leave there for my aunts, odds and ends that we no longer use but will find a second chance home somewhere in Lima. Our outdated, worn clothes will breathe new life in the third world country where my parents were born and raised.

Bianca waddles into the room wearing Barney pajamas. "Mama, where are you doin'?" She walks over to the suitcase and stuffs random things into the side pockets. "I help, what's next?"

"Oh thank you so much, *mamita*, you're a good helper!" Bianca is two almost three, she is well behaved and makes us all gush with pride, especially Papi. Bianca is his pride and joy, his everything. I don't know what he would do if anything were ever to separate them.

"¿Ya estas lista?" Papi asks, looking at his watch. Always one to be on time, a rare specimen, he should be on display in a museum with a golden plaque reading: **A Punctual Latino.** *"Vamos que empiesa trafico si no salimos ahora."* Looking tired and agitated he turns his attention to Bianca. His bloodshot eyes indicate that he had a restless sleep last night.

"*Ya*, I'm ready," Lorena replies grabbing last minute things and stuffing them in her already bloated handbag. She tries to grab the suitcase off the bed, Papi grabs for the overweight luggage and groans.

"¿Que tienes aquí, la refrigeradora?" Papi jokes with her.

We join them outside as they pack up the car. With Bianca in my arms and Guille by my side we say our goodbyes. Lorena reminds me of the frozen prepared meals she left so that we wouldn't starve in her absence; healthy meals from A to Z; **A**ji de Gallina to **Z**apallo soup. Watching them drive away, I wish I would have known that this was going to be the last time we would be together as a family.

Guille, Bianca, and I lounge in our pajamas all morning watching Pocahontas and Toy Story, while I was on the phone with Emilio for most of the time. He wanted to come see me but there was definitely a rule about not having boys in the house while no one was home. That was spelled out clearly to me.

Bored, I decide to pack up the kids and go to Yvette's house, which was just a short walk down South Quaker Lane.

Reaching her house I open the front door and call out, "¿Yvette, donde estas?!" My voice echoing through the empty house we find the clan in the backyard.

"*Coño*, Yvette! At least try to ash in the ashtray. ¡*Si tu Papa te coja fumando!*" Yvette's petite mother bellows in a loud voice. She is tiny, plump and attractive; a female with an air of refinement and a twist of drunken sailor's mouth. Yvette's family moved from D.R. when her mom started developing boobs. Her father was afraid the ruthless dictator Trujillo would lay eyes on his beautiful daughter and they fled out of fear that he would call her to the *palacio* for "*una visita*". Trujillo went through young Dominican girls like *mondongo*. So they packed up their *platos* and *platanos* and fled to Washington Heights, the Santo Domingo of New York. That is where she met her first and only boyfriend, Yvette's father. He made sure to get her while she was still young, unspoiled, and naïve.

Guille disappears into the crowd of running boys playing tag while I pull up a chair with Bianca on my lap, moving a purse that is on the chair to the steps behind me.

"You hungry *mija*? There's some leftover *mangu* in the kitchen," Yvette's mom offers.

"I'm always hungry." I look down at Bianca who nods her head too. I grab her up on my hip and head to the kitchen.

Yvette's father marches in, clearing his throat. Always kind and respectful to me, I try to be courteous towards him despite the horror stories the girls tell me about him. The girls grew up with a father who openly criticized them all their lives, clearly affecting their self-esteem. Comments about their weight caused them grief, and remarks about their academic performance at school made them feel inadequate. His open, constant infidelity to their mother also did not sit well with the girls. Inheriting the cheating gene from his ancestors, he was as loyal as a bunny rabbit.

"Hello, nice to see you," I offer as he grabs a glass and opens the closet where he stashes his liquor.

"*¿Hola Ady, como estas?*" he mumbles in a deep baritone voice. Yvette's father is a handsome older man. He is physically fit and looks like he could be on a Spanish soap opera (or not, usually the only darkies on the novellas are the help). His face is devoid of any wrinkles to give a warning sign of his real age. The only indication of his refinement is covered by a very convincing, very expensive, hairpiece that he never takes off. He sleeps with it like a mummy, covering it with an Aunt Jemima head wrap.

Quickly grabbing my plate I hurry back outside whispering to Yvette, "Your daddy is drinking the Brugal!" That Dominican Rum is so watered down by now we are surprised he hasn't called the Brugal factory in DR to complain. After chugging down the harsh rum, we would replace it with water or apple juice.

"Thought you were going to go see your mom this weekend," Yvette leans in and shouts over the loud conversations around us. She remembers everything, things I don't seem to remember myself. She is my personal rolodex and appointment calendar (maybe the weed is affecting me more than I care to admit).

"Guess not, she didn't call me to say she was going to come scoop me." My mother still seems to be a shattered image of who she was before. From what I can tell, by the very few times she does pick me up, she is still unhappy and drinking heavily. I never have the courage to tell her she needs help. *Sweep it under the carpet and don't look at it, so that we can pretend that it doesn't exist.* I think this might be the reason she doesn't pick me up very often. On my part I don't push for her to pick me up. I feel horrible for having abandoned my sister in such terrible conditions.

The last time I was at the house I got into an argument with Joseph about some silly shit. He ended the heated conversation with, "That's why I don't expect much from you. You'll be pregnant and on welfare by the time you are seventeen!" He laughed in my face and walked away. In the heat of the moment, in all my eloquence, all I could come up with was, "Ffffuck you, fucker!!"

Bianca grabs a nearby basketball and brings it to me, so I take a seat on the floor and we roll it back and forth.

"Let's go do something," Vanessa, Yvette's older sister, whines. Vanessa is the sister who got pregnant at thirteen. She is the wild child that smokes, drinks, and obviously has unprotected sex. She is a firecracker who always needs to be occupied. Her beauty is overshadowed by the insecurity that her daddy nicely infused in each of the girls. Four years older than us, her only friends are her sisters. She has trust issues and does not have any interest in having friends. "Connecticut is so boring, there's nothing to do. Nothing ever happens here." Looking back, I wish that she could have been right.

I finish polishing off my plate of *mangu*, boiled green plantains topped with sautéed onions and fried cheese, salami and eggs. Yvette's father comes waltzing outside with his glass of non-alcoholic apple juice, looking down on everyone from the porch. Not saying much, he puts the damper on our party. With the mood ruined, I say my goodbyes and Yvette joins me to walk us halfway to the house.

Besides Yvette and Nicki, I also chill with a few other people from Conard on a daily basis. April, lives in a church run program for teen mothers. Saint Agnes provides child care for a group of young girls who want to stay in school and hopefully graduate. April is a white, skinny blonde with an appetite for drama. She is always ready to defend who she is with her smart mouth and heavy fists. Pete is her Puerto Rican Prince Charming who provides her with the three P's: *Puños*, Pregnancies and Problems. In between all the drama, she is my loyal smoking buddy. She moved into an apartment in Hartford with Pete during our sophomore year. I was the only guest to attend their wedding. One night after the three of us smoked a fat blunt, Pete asked her to marry him. With a cheesy smile, he walked into the kitchen and grabbed a broom he carefully laid on the ground. As they jumped the broom, hand in hand, they vowed to be together "till death do they part" as I clapped and threw cooked rice and beans at them. Keeping his word, almost a decade after they married, he went to jail for 10 to 15 for beating her "almost to death".

Another one of my after school buddies, Juan, is the sweetest, most religious Puerto Rican I ever met. He is guided by his faith but was influenced to stray from his morals a few times, as any normal teenager would. For the most part when I chill with Juan we have fun without being high. Like they say, he gets his high from Jesus. Curious about what motivated Juan, Yvette and I attended one of his services in a tiny Pentecostal church off of Park Street one day. The service was filled with loud music and even louder praise. There were women with long skirts and longer hair crying, laughing, and holding their hands up towards the sky. Instead of "getting the Holy Ghost, *Espiritu Santo*" I "got the giggles". I don't know if the laughter I had to hold back was a nervous laughter or if I truly felt that this was all a scam. Sitting in a crowd of true believers I felt like a phony. Smiling politely and trying not to express my disinterest, I glanced sideways at Yvette and her equally fake smile. Was I condemned to go to what they described as hell because I felt more divine elation from listening to John Lennon's "Imagine"? I still believed myself to be a good person even though I didn't drop to the floor and start speaking in tongues. I was not sure how Juan could still keep his faith fifteen years later when it was His divine plan to take away the life of his son before his time. *Just a baby.*

"Papi home!" Bianca squeals running to the door from the window.

As Papi walks in, the familiar smell of cigarette smoke and cough drops fills the house. He bends down as Bianca runs to him almost knocking him down. Giving me a kiss, he goes to the kitchen and picks up the phone. Pulling out a calling card, he calls my aunts in Peru to tell them that Lorena's flight departed on time, as well as flight numbers and arrival times. Shouting into the phone, he soon turns to me and gives me a look, as if asking me if I want to say hello. I give him a polite shake of the head and a wave hello as I duck out of sight. There is nothing I hate more than talking to my grandmother and aunts in Peru.

It's not that I don't like hearing from them, I just hate third world communication. I always feel like I am talking into a broken toy phone with the time delay, conversations get meshed together like a conversation between two inebriated people. When I am forced to talk, like on someone's birthday or anniversary, I close my eyes and picture we are underwater talking on a tin can phone. A unique technology reserved for people who live in third world luxury.

Hanging up the phone, Papi pulls out pre-prepared dishes from the fridge.

"¿*Tienen hambre?*" he questions as we are all sprawled out on the couch.

"Yeah, a little."

"I'm starving."

"I hungry."

We all pick out what we want from the buffet Lorena packed up and labeled in Tupperware.

"Can I just have a hot dog?" Guille whines, not finding anything appetizing.

"*¿Toda esta comida y quieres comer un hot dog? No, comes lo que hay.*" Papi says sternly, pointing out the fact that hot dogs are not on the menu for today.

"I'm not hungry then." Guille says retreating to the living room.

Papi loudly clears his throat. When Papi gets annoyed, that noise is like the crack of a belt. All he has to do is clear his throat to display his disapproval. Hearing Papi's clearing of the throat, Guille decides against not sitting at the table with us. He grabs a plate of white rice and Peruvian French Fries (they look like

McDonald's fries on steroids sprinkled with Adobo) and reluctantly sits down to eat with us.

I eagerly down my plate of *Causa*, a Peruvian version of lasagna, layers of mashed potato, black olives, onion, chilies, olive oil and tuna fish; one of my favorites. Peruvian cuisine has more potatoes in it than Idaho. Owning the bragging rights for growing more than 2,000 varieties of potatoes, Peruvian chefs, dice, slice, mash, shred and boil potatoes till they scream for mercy. My *Causa* is causing my stomach to squeal for April. *No questionable sloppy Joes for me!* I feel sorry for people who have to go home and eat dry meat loaf and rice pilaf. Come to my house and partake in our banging-ass-food.

Like I mentioned before, Peruvian cuisine is not easy on the eyes. When you look at a dish it is not love at first sight but once it hits your mouth, you're done, and like a bad drug habit you keep coming back for more. Even NASA has tapped in to our incredibly delicious and nourishing menu. Since the 80's astronauts have been taking foods like quinoa, kiwicha and maca into outer space with them. It's not rocket science: Peruvian food is off the hook.

In between bites, I contemplate how I am going to approach Papi with my newest proposition. Nicki is finally making enough profit off of her weed to afford moving out of her house. She paints a picture of living on our own with no one to answer to so clearly that I actually see our nicely decorated apartment in my head. Nicki already secured an apartment, conveniently located off of Park Street on Park Terrace. She said he offered her a two bedroom apartment for only $500 a month. I just have to convince Papi that it would be beneficial to all of us if I move out on my own.

"Do you have to pay taxes on an apartment? I mean if you rent an apartment, does the government charge you taxes?" I throw out, trying to start a conversation that I hope will end up with Papi sending me off and wishing me the best of luck with my newfound independence. I start to sweat and I soon lose my appetite.

"¿Porque preguntas?" Papi asks in suspicion already.

"Oh, I don't know, it's just that Nicki is moving out of her house soon and I was wondering if she is going to have to pay taxes, too."

"*Pobre chica, no viene de una familia quien lo cuide,*" Papi replies, as if he knows where this talk is headed. *I, on the other hand, come from a family that clearly provides me with everything I need.*

"She no have mommy?" Bianca investigates, too wise for her years. She has tiny pieces of white rice all over her face and is sporting a milk mustache.

"She has a mom. It's not like she kicked her out of the house, she *wants* to move out. She is moving into a nice apartment in Hartford." Stretching the truth like Laughy Taffy, truth is the apartment is in a bad neighborhood where drug dealers outnumber the roaches on the block. "It's a two bedroom apartment," I add, about ready to blurt it out.

"*¿Y como va ha pagar la renta? ¿Ella consigo trabajo?*"

"She has money in the bank." I lie about where her income is truly coming from.

"*Ella ya tiene que pensar como va pagar luz, electricidad, comida, calefacción, gas. Hay un montón de cosas que uno no piensa cuando están viviendo con los padres.*" Papi rambles on, standing up to clear the table before he's even done listing all the different bills that come with having your own place.

No, sit back down; I'm not finished yet! The words echo in my mind as I jump up, grab the plates, and quickly dump them in the sink. Sitting back down I see Papi is tired and ready to get up from the table.

"So since she has another room she asked me if I wanted to move in with her," I blurt out in one quick breath. The moment I look at Papi for a reaction, I wish I hadn't. The look on Papi's face is one of hurt and disappointment like someone just punched him in the stomach.

Guille rolls his eyes at me and gets up from the table, while Bianca follows him to the living room, chicken drum in hand.

That awkward silence lingers for a while, as I sit and look out the sliding glass door, awaiting a response. *What!? It's not like I told him I was pregnant, I'm not a drug addict, I'm not dropping out of school! I simply asked if I could move out on my own.*

Taking a breath, he stands up from the table and clears his throat. "*Mamita, tu eres inteligente y creo que puedes hacer ese decisión tu mismo. Dejame saber lo que quieres hacer.*" He walks away, leaving the decision in my trembling hands.

Boring Old White Folks

I am sitting at a crossroad, I look to the right and see freedom, to the left I see my family and a structured life I am not sure I want to follow. Little did I know then that my decision would be made for me in the very near future.

"Let's go people!" Mr. Maybe, the chunky, red faced Social Studies teacher, yells as we stare back at him unresponsively. We are crowded at a table devouring our snacks during one of our many breaks. I am now part of a program called "Connections" at Conard, the only group that gets the privilege of coming to the cafeteria in between classes for munchies (besides the special needs kids; the drooling kind, not the ones with behavioral issues like us). "Connections" is a pathway to graduation for students stuck in the middle; the ones who have trouble in mainstream classes but are not extreme enough that they will drop out of school. In years past, it was a sort of holding cell for students who needed a place to wait until they decided to drop out. Keeping our group of 25 confined from mainstream classes and pairing us up with only four teachers made us focus on getting shit done.

As the group files out of the cafeteria like soldiers, Yvette, Lynn, and I straggle behind.

"Let's go check out what they are doing at the bleachers," I suggest, not wanting to sit in a coma-like state while The Great Gatsby is being read aloud; he is not the Great Anything in my life.

We quickly duck into the girls' bathroom just as one of the security guards turns the corner.

Hiding in the bathroom, each one of us in our own stalls, we wait until the security guard passes. As soon as the coast is clear, Lynn spreads the contents of her book bag out on the counter. She begins her beauty regimen as me and Yvette look on.

"What you don't have in your book bag?" Yvette teases, playing with an eyelash curler.

"Books," I joke, "and a pencil."

Lynn digs into the bottom of her book bag and pulls out a pencil.

"Eyeliner don't count."

"It's still a writing tool," she retorts, looking at my reflection in the mirror. She is redoing her long, black pin straight hair. She is a pretty girl with low self-esteem who focuses way too much on her minor acne and non-existent boobs. Lucky for her, with age comes clear skin and enough money in her savings account to pay for a nicely done boob job. But for now, she is caking on the make-up like a geisha mask.

Making our way to the bleachers while trying to avoid the teachers and security, I hear the theme song from Mission Impossible in my head. We arrive to the masses on the bleachers, where I spot Emilio's familiar face. He gives me a quick peck on the lips. Now that me and Emilio are officially dating I have to deal with Maya and her nasty attitude. She stares me down in the hallways and loudly whispers to whoever is around what she thinks of me. She tells people that she is still messing around with Emilio, which I eventually find to be true. Maya is one of the biggest problems I had in my life at the time. I should have considered myself to be very fortunate, completely oblivious to current events outside of my backyard; the Rwandan genocide has taken place not even a few months prior. The screams and wailing of women and children are muted on my radar, tuned into things like gossip and teenage drama. I am contemplating leaving my family, as babies are being ripped out of their mother's lifeless arms over 7,000 miles away. *100 days, 500,000 dead.*

"Dead, dead, dead! I need to charge my phone. I can't get calls, shit!" Cutty's complaints cut into my thoughts, and I look over to see him shaking his big grey cell phone as if that can charge the battery. Back in the day, before people were born with cell phones in their hands, Cutty was one of the only kids in school who owned a cell phone. He never advertised what he did to afford that luxury, but everyone knew what he sold to buy his nice toys.

After a few tokes of a cigarette we get up to make our way back to class using the back stairwells, hoping to get to our classroom without anyone seeing us. Mission Impossible again, only this time it doesn't go as well.

"Ladies, where are you headed?" Recognizing the deep baritone voice that echoes from the bottom of the stairwell, we all groan and freeze in mid-stride.

"Just going back to class after break, Ms. Muffo," I answer politely. Ms. Muffo our gym teacher very much looks the part; she has huge muscles and not an ounce of fat on her body. Her bowl cut and deep voice makes you do a double take. Resembling a teenage boy, students constantly mark her with a big red L with no solid proof if she is truly a lesbian or not.

"You should be with your class then, not in the hallways in between class time," she pronounces with groomed authority. "I'll walk you three to your classroom."

Making our way to the third floor, Yvette comments in Spanish, *"Esta pata, siempre molestando."*

"Es porque somos Hispanos." I declare, eyeing a white girl walking down the hall in our direction.

"Hi Ms. Muffo!" The girl squeals as she gives a wave, long blonde hair bouncing with her every step.

"Hi Caitlin," Ms. Muffo replies casually, not bothering to grill her about where she is supposed to be.

"*Viste, que cojones!*" Yvette chimes in, stating the obvious.

"Ladies, didn't your parents teach you that it is very rude to speak Spanish when in the presence of non-Spanish speakers?" Ms. Muffo looks towards Lynn for agreement, but Lynn shrugs her shoulders and puts her hands up, not wanting to take sides.

"Uh, no, my parents don't speak English so that would be very hard for them not to do," I retort. It's a lie, but she would never know, she doesn't frequent the same places as my parents anyways.

"Well I do speak English very well, so I am telling you," She adds as we reach our classroom.

Ms. Muffo knocks a little too loudly with her man hands, until our math teacher comes to the door with a look of disapproval.

"I think these belong to you," Ms. Muffo states dryly to Ms. Enfintino.

Still standing at the door in between the two teachers I fake a cough, disguising the word "Pata" loud enough for the class to hear. Even with only a handful of Hispanics in the group, the black and white kids learned enough Spanish to understand what I'd just said. Most of the students start snickering and people are laughing behind the shields of their books. The only two in the room who don't get the joke are the teachers at our sides. Never bothering to learn a word of Spanish, they are oblivious to our prepubescent humor.

"Ladies, thank you for making time in your busy schedule to make it to class. You can all stay after school today to make up the missing class time," Ms. Enfintino says as she shuts the door. Cutting our attempt at excuses short, she ushers us to our seats with a loud hush. Her pale, pasty, white skin rivals Ms. Branich's who was probably born with see-through skin. Both teachers sport short unattractive haircuts in different hues of blonde. Looking like paper doll cutouts, they fit the mold of what a teacher looks like at Conard. No Bill Cosby or Gloria Estefan educator look-alikes here. *Hey hey hey!*

Our English teacher, Ms. Branich, is going over the chapter summary of the Great Gatsby.

Ms. Vranich questions the room, "What symbolism did you see within the themes that ran throughout the novel?"

The classroom is so quiet you could hear a bag of weed drop.

"Come on you guys, what differences do you see between Nick and Gatsby?"

Ms. Enfintino chimes in from the back of the room, "What about the clash between old money and new money?"

My body is here but my mind is not, I have no idea what answer they are desperately searching for. I skimmed the book at home: Ivy League colleges, lavish parties, estates, millionaires, golf, mansions? What did Fitzgerald know about a Peruvian-American living in Connecticut in 1995? This guy was probably a freaking racist. Why are we analyzing this garbage that he wrote like a hundred years ago? These characters are a million miles away from who I am right now, sitting at my desk staring out the window. I will never be sitting in a huge mansion of my own in this lifetime. This book is not relevant to my life; this book is horse shit.

Turning my head, and raising my hand slowly, I glance at Ms. Branich with a look of innocence and throw out, "What about the clash of people with *nada-* money?"

"What do you mean by *nada-* money?" She mimics, getting red in the face.

"You know, people like us that have *not-a*-dime."

Getting the reaction I want from my classmates, they all burst into a roar of laughter.

"Yeah, where da Puerto Rican's at during the Roaring Twenties?" Someone shouts from the back row.

"Did Puerto Ricans own estates too?"

"Did Gatsby have black servants?"

The questions keep whizzing like bullets as Ms. Branich stands in front of the class, silent and at a loss for words. Her tight lips signal she is getting frustrated with our antics, and I immediately feel bad. She is a cool teacher and she truly cares about us and has a passion for literature. I am embarrassed for her and ashamed that I started such retaliation but I'm saved by the bell again, and it is time to switch classes. As I get up to leave, Ms. Enfintino steps into my path.

"That was done in very poor taste. Not reading the material is not an excuse to goof off," she whispers, close to my face. Ms. Enfintino has the most atrocious breath you will ever, ever experience. Every time she speaks, you are forced to turn your head. The students joke that she has oatmeal mixed with shit every morning for breakfast. *Poor taste*, your breath must *taste poor*.

"Uh, huh. I will read for tomorrow and see what happens to Gatsby. I hope he doesn't die, he seems reckless," I say to please her, turning around and bumping right into Ms. Branich.

"Sorry Ms. Branich," I offer with sincerity, keeping my eyes to the floor.

"That's okay sweetie. I know you were just stating the obvious. If you truly want to sit here and read a book about people like you, with *nada* money, wake up and do something about it," she says with a genuine smile, "I would use it in my classroom. Until then we will have to sit in class and read about old, boring, white folks like me."

She gave me the power of words that day and then she gave me direction. She gave the Chavo to my Ocho. The Bang to my Chitty Chitty. The Willy to my Wonka. The Calle to my 13. Me dio el fuego ese dia para escribir.

Stoned in Jamaica

When tragic moments occur in life, it all feels like a blur. If you ever had the privilege of getting high, you are familiar with the feeling of everything around you moving in slow motion. The world seems to slow on its axis until you get down from your high. Is that why everyone in Jamaica is so chill? Things get done when they get done; don't have a shit fit, no need to rush. The next episode of my life is a mix of being stoned in Jamaica while simultaneously having the vinyl record of my life grind abruptly to an annoying, scratching halt. In a thick Jamaican accent, *"Rewind!"*

That morning I wake up and the earth stands still. Had I known what was to come, I would have stayed in our nice new home *all day*. I would have taken *a thousand* long, hot, showers. I would have snuggled in my nice warm sheets *for hours*. I would have *paid attention* in all my classes. I would have breathed in the fresh air *a million* times that day. I would have told Lorena *not to go* on that trip...

But of course I didn't know.

"*Mamita*, I have to talk to you." Papi turns to me while I am grabbing a drink from the fridge. He is looking at me with bloodshot eyes, and I wonder why he is not dressed for work yet. He never calls out, not even on the rare occasions when he gets sick.

"What's wrong?" I ponder, thinking for sure that this is the conversation where he is going to tell me I have to move back with my mom, since I am still getting into trouble here. After deciding, on my own that moving out with Nicki would be too difficult for me right now, I flushed that idea down the toilet a few days after I asked. *I don't want to leave. I promise I will try harder.*

Leaving Bianca and Guille inside watching TV, we make our way to the back deck. Sitting down at the tiny patio table and pulling out a Marlboro, Papi lets out a big long sigh, and I have a flashback to when Lorena offered me a cigarette.

"Okay... Ahhh. Well, I am not sure what to do and I need your help," he begins, lighting up his cigarette. *This means some serious bananas.* Papi only speaks to me in English when serious matters are being discussed. He is sitting there thinking hard about what he is going to say next, as I look out at the horizon to see the sun setting quickly. The sky is an egg splatter of red, orange and purple.

"Lorena is leaving," he reports in a whisper.

"Leaving Peru... today?" I am confused. Lorena is still in Peru she didn't come back yet.

"Leaving *me.*" he pauses, "She called a few days ago and said that she needs to sort out some issues. She told me that she wants to move back to Peru... with Pachi."

Pachi... his name vibrates in my mind like a swear word. Although I never met him before I have a lot of sentiments reserved for him. Lorena married him and eventually left him years later. She never speaks about it but I always picture him verbally abusing her, getting drunk, and frightening her and Guille when he was a baby. Alone and scared, I see her fleeing Peru to forget about him and start a new life in the U.S. This is what I believed to be true as the real truth, only Lorena and Pachi know.

What I do know is that Pachi was supposed to be her past. Although I never met him before, Pachi was my blood; actually Pachi was my second cousin.

It wasn't supposed to happen like this. Lorena told me she needed a place to stay and Papi had extra room in his apartment for her and Guille. She took up the offer to stay with Pachi's uncle in Connecticut and the rest was like any other love story. They tried to fight it at first, but I guess love always triumphs.

As their love grew, so did the secrecy. Their love was unconventional, inappropriate and unexpected. Family in Peru would definitely disapprove of their relationship. So they decided to keep their relationship under the radar like a Japanese Fu-Go balloon, unobserved and dangerous. Phone calls to Peru left out the details of their living arrangements. Pictures sent home showed no hand holding or loving embraces. When Bianca was born there were no colorful birth announcements sent out. She was brought into this world a beautiful secret.

This trip to Lima was supposed to be the beginning of Lorena and Papi's life together without the secrecy. The trip was a mission to get legally divorced from Pachi so that they could move on and finally let the family in Peru know that they were together and in love.

"Love... is such a strange thing," Papi remarks out loud.

"What does that mean, so she just doesn't love you anymore? I don't understand how she can do this. What is going to happen? Is she going to say goodbye and come look you in the eyes or is she going to just send for her things?" I am frantic, asking one question after another and not giving Papi a chance to answer.

"I don't know what Lorena is feeling right now. I don't know what our future looks like," he finally responds as the sun begins to set behind him. I feel like we are racing against the sunset. We need to come to a resolution before the sun disappears, or else we will be stranded with no plan sitting in the dark.

"So she's just leaving like that? Bianca and Guille... what happens to them?"

"She is coming home to get them and their things. That leaves just you and me. Mama, I won't be hurt if you decide that you want to go back and live with your mother. All I know is that I am not going to be able to afford the mortgage on the house if Lorena is not here. We are going to lose the house."

Papi doesn't seem to be mad, just confused in a daze and heartbroken. What did Papi do to have this happen to him and why is Papi asking *me* for help? I have no clue what we should do. I'm only sixteen, why do I have to contemplate this?

"I don't know Papi," I say in a panic, "I want to stay with you. I am sorry that I have been getting into so much trouble at school. What are we going to do?"

"I don't know. Things are getting bad at work. They are trying to make me quit to get someone younger in there. Even if I am able to save my job this house is going to go into foreclosure and with all the things we put on the credit cards for the house and the car loan... it doesn't look good. I'm going to have to declare bankruptcy either way *mamita*."

This is too much for me. I feel like puking and laughing and crying all at the same time. Fighting back hot tears I get up from the table, holding onto the railing of the deck I stare into the pitch black. I look up and glare at the full moon. It seems to be holding my stare awaiting a reasonable resolution from me. *Goodnight Moon.*

After a long, quiet, tranquil, pause Papi gets up, hugs me, and asks with tears in his eyes, "How about… what if. Do you maybe… want to go live in Peru?"

I am- Soy

Paddington Bear was from "Darkest Peru". Deepest... darkest... Peru. Sounds like the last place someone would want to pack up and relocate to. The year before, I had visited Peru for the first time in my life. As the plane hit the dirt runway in Lima the passengers broke into a loud applause. I was confused whether they were applauding the fact that we were in Peru, or the fact that we were still alive after the terrifyingly bumpy landing. As we walked out of the airport the dust, smog, and garbage fumes smacked us in the face full force. We visited my grandmother's house in Lima and we were welcomed by a crowd of family made up of cousins we'd never met before, and aunts and uncles we only knew by phone calls and pictures.

After a crash course in family tree-ology, a group of us took an old dilapidated plane north to Cuzco to visit Machu Picchu, one of the new Seven Wonders of the World. Boarding an ancient train that seemed too old to take on the mountain, we started our ascent into the heavens. After what seemed like a thousand hours, we finally reached the ancient ruins perched atop the 8,000 foot mountain where I broke away from my group and walked out to an open field. With the breathtaking view and the excitement of thousands of tourist I picked a nice patch of grass, laid down on my back and stared up at the sky. There was an unexplainable energy that radiated out of the ground and into my outstretched body. *What the hell was that?* Inca power seemed to be trapped in the ruins and the ground below me. I got up quickly, freaked out that the ground was somehow going to devour me.

I don't remember why I said yes to Papi. Maybe it was the energy I had felt atop Machu Picchu that was calling me back to my motherland. Whatever it was, Papi and I were making the big move to deepest, darkest, Peru.

"So you're moving to... Lima? Lima, Peru... in South America?" My guidance counselor Mrs. Jackson, trying to extract the whole story from me, asks, "What's up?" Mrs. Jackson is the only cool white woman I know. When we talk she doesn't make stupid assumptions. She speaks to me, not down to me. Though she looks like a cookie cutter version of the rest of the faculty at Conard, she has one bonus point in my eyes: she is married to an equally cool, handsome black man.

"I dunno, we just decided to move," I mumble, not in a mood to talk about what is really happening at home. I am nervous and not sure if I made the right choice.

"So how are you feeling about this?" She shrugs, reclining back in her chair, making me feel like she has all the time in the world for me.

"Don't know... nervous, excited, I guess." The truth is I don't really know what I should be feeling. I am in limbo right now, just going through the motions: go to school, chill, eat, sleep, wake up, do it again. My life is just blah right now and I need to find that motivation soon or I am afraid I will end up like those *viejas* on Park Street. Mad at the world because they missed the boat when they were young enough to jump on it. I am looking for something but I don't even know if I would recognize it if I found it.

"Who are you going with?" She is trying to pry open the safe box that I have under lock and key.

"Just me and Papi," I am about ready to burst into tears and tell her the whole story. "My step-mom..."

"Your step-mom?" Ms. Jackson inquires with raised eyebrows.

"I don't know... but I gotta get to class," I quickly say as I grab my book bag and turn to leave her office.

"Wait, here is my home address," she interrupts me, "When you get a chance, write to me and let me know how you are doing." She hands me her business card with her home address written on the back.

"Okay," I nod, putting it in my back pocket. "Take care Ms. Jackson," I add, giving her a tight hug.

As I walk out Ms. Jackson stands at her office door with her arms crossed. "Hey Ady, you know what the shortest complete sentence in the English language is?"

Thinking for a few second I shake my head no.

"I am." She says with a smile, "Think about it and pack that in your suitcase."

I am?

I am.

I am...

"Punks jump up to get beat down," she sings as she walks by me with a Cheshire cat smile across her lips. Spitting lyrics from Brand Nubian, she kills the vocalizations but gets her point across the hallway as she stares intimidatingly at me. Maya is on one side of the hallway with her sister and friends, and I am on the other with Nicki and Yvette. I am cleaning out the locker that was mine, but became the communal locker since I had prime real estate; right in the middle of the intersection on the first floor, the chill spot in between classes.

"Gross!" I shriek finding a black, decomposing apple stuck to a notebook in the bottom of the locker.

"There it is," Nicki laughs "I was going to show Boobie how we smoked out of an apple dat day. He said that was some white people voodoo."

"You weren't complaining when we got high that day." Yvette chimes in, helping me clean out the locker.

"Hey, whatever gets you there," I retort, looking out of the corner of my eye as Emilio walks with Maya down the hall.

"FIGHT!!!" We hear someone yell a few minutes later. Everyone jumps into action and runs to where the commotion is taking place a few feet from my locker. Excited with a break from the everyday routine, a fight is like an unrehearsed circus performance. Fights usually occur between girls and almost always black and Hispanic girls. You hardly ever see a mess of blond hair and blood in these hallways. Maybe white girls have better communication skills. The girls that are throwing it down in front of us are ruthless.

Trying to get a better look I jump on Yvette's back and get some height above the mob. I recognize one of the contenders, Raquel, who is beating on Maya like a rug. Maya is being dragged by her long, black, pin straight hair down to the ground and she is screaming bloody murder. It should have been no contest since the girl that is fighting Maya is skinny as a rail and shorter than a sentence, but she is whoopin' ass.

I see Emilio and Cutty break into the circle and assume they are both going to defend Maya. But Emilio grabs the other girl and pulls her off of Maya while Cutty goes up to Maya and grabs her in a choke hold. Maya manages to grab her shoe and stabs Cutty on the side of the face with her heel. Grabbing her by the face, he mushes her to the ground.

The security guards swarm in trying to break the human chain that is surrounding the fight. Taking the two girls away after the fact, they walk away acting like they think they were the heroes that stopped the bloodbath somehow.

"What the hell was that?" I declare as I jump down from Yvette's back.

"Dunno, I do know that Raquel is Cutty's sister and you don't mess with family."

"What? They never talk to each other; they don't even look at each other!" I'm surprised, but neither of them seem to question it.

Throwing everything back into my locker, we make our way to the cafeteria.

"I'm going to the Puerto Rican day parade this weekend, y'all want to roll?" Nicki throws out.

"Do I look like I want to be surrounded by a group of loud, drunk Puerto Ricans?" Yvette jokes as we wait in line.

"Where, what's it for?" I ask, even though I know that I can't go anyways because I have to pack.

"Hartford. Why you mean what it's for? It's just a damn parade." Nicki grabs a bag of Doritos and tosses them in her book bag. I wonder how much it would be if we totaled all the things we stole on a yearly basis. I think it would be a small fortune.

"What y'all celebrating? Usually when you have parades it's because you are celebrating some kinda event. Independence, someone famous birthday, shit like that." I grab a bag of cookies, brownies, and a muffin, quickly stuffing them in the pockets of my hoodie.

"We celebratin' our Puertoricaness and how we are the bomb, that's what," she says with a laugh, rectifying the numerous Puerto Rican parades that take place a year.

Grabbing a seat next to Evelyn and a few other girls, we sit down to our feast of trans fat and high fructose corn syrup. Breaking open the plastic seals on my lunch I quickly demolish my brownie, I am famished.

"Damn, Ady, eat much?" Juan points to all the empty wrappers on the table.

"I'm starving." I shrug chomping on my cookies. "Don't you know, stressed spelled backwards is desserts? I don't know if I want to move but we can't stay here. What the hell am I going to do in Peru? It's a third world country. What does that even mean?"

"You gotta think three times before you do anything. Before you walk outside, before you eat the food, before you drink the water," Juan jokes, trying to make me laugh.

"I'm scared that we are going to move there and I am going to hate it," I say, licking my thumb, "Then I am going to be stranded in a place where I don't know anybody."

"I bet they don't have Doritos in Peru." Nicki proclaims, dragging her Dorito through a mound of ketchup.

"Doritos are universal, I'm sure they have them or something like them. If you don't like it... shit... just come back." Yvette shrugs her shoulders. She makes it sound so simple. *Just come back.*

I don't want to say goodbye to anyone so I quietly walk out through the back door instead. I am now able to breathe and by the time I get home I am satisfied with my decision that now doesn't seem like the end of the world. Coming to a quiet peace knowing that my decision can always take another turn, I am ready to make my journey to the third world.

Gringo

So this stage of my life will be completely in Spanish…. *Si en español.*

¡Y no el spanglish que hablamos en los Estados! ¡Por favor! No, estoy hablando del Castellano de los Españoles quienes vinieron en sus barcos con sus trajes blancos, bien planchados. El español…espérate, creo que hemos perdido la mitad de la gente que no habla español. Los americanos, los gringos, que no les importan si pueden comunicarse con sus jardineros o la sirvienta (gracias a la feísima Dame Edna, Vanity Fair, Febrero 2003). Esos puertorriqueños, que dicen que son boricuas pero nunca en sus vidas han tocado su propia tierra, los mismos que no saben escribir o leer español. Los africanos que conversan en como diez diferentes idiomas pero nunca los escuchas hablando en español. (¿Por lo menos pueden tratar de aprender un idiomita mas, no crees?) Lo siento en el alma, pero creo que tengo que modificar esto un poco y ser traidor a mi lengua materna.

You win; sorry I lost you for a minute back there. So you are going to have to stretch your mind and *pretend* that this stage of my life is completely in Spanish. Jorge Ramos, Univision, Spanish, not Fat Joe got marbles in your mouth type Spanish. The Spanish that makes you feel like you never knew Spanish to begin with. The "mira's", "verdad's" and the "que que's" quietly linger in the background embarrassed by their constant use. So get out your Spanish/ English dictionary because we are going to the Republic of Peru…

"A journey of a thousand miles must begin with a single step." That was easy for Lao-tzu to declare. Legend holds that he was born with white hair having spent more than eighty years in his mother's womb. He *walked* out of his mother's womb an old master! (Chinese history, look it up.) Taoist belief proclaims there are three jewels to be sought in one's life: Compassion,

Moderation and Humility. My capacity for compassion equated to, "Oh man! You got your kicks dirty! That sucks." My definition of moderation was, "I'm straight, I'm hurt already", while passing the bottle of Hennessey. My humility was the only gem that got passed down to me from my parents. I had some remnants of humbleness in my possession (as much as a spoiled teenage American can scrape up).

I look out of the 9 by 12 windowpane down below to what would be my future. The lights of Lima blink like a Lite Brite under our plane. In my head I hear the instrumental version of "El Condor Pasa", the traditional Andean music that plays when you see documentaries on the Discovery Channel about Machu Picchu. You know, the one where they are playing the zampona, the tiny little flute that Peter Pan stole from us and Disney gave us no credit for? The song that Simon and Garfunkel remade in the 70's, "If I Could". If you still don't know the song that is running through my head you need to widen your interests (or just hide in your computer again and YouTube it... "El Condor Pasa").

"You okay?" Papi looks at me as we wait for the Peruvian mafia to grab their luggage from the overhead compartments. These little old ladies are rough, they be throwing elbows.

"Yeah, I'm good, just tired and hungry," I reply, eyeing a little girl who is holding a see-through gift bag with a ridiculously huge amount of Reese's peanut butter cups. *They don't have Reese's in Peru?*

Making our way off the plane, we walk into the unventilated airport. Papi carries my book bag and his carry-on bag. As I wait in line, empty handed, I stare at a huge mural of Machu Picchu with a condor overhead, wings spread wide. Funny how birds seem to always correlate with places. If you see a crane you think of Japan. A toucan can make you think Amazon rainforest.

Flamingos are from Florida. A huge ostrich, automatically Australia. Bald Eagle, naturally North America. A peacock, perhaps India. Dodo bird, definitely Alice in Wonderland, and when you think of Peru a condor is pictured. The Andean condor, vulture gryphus, commonly known as... the vulture!

The national symbol of my heritage! A freakin' vulture, a dirty scavenger that feeds off the remains of the poor, wounded, and decaying. A bird with no voice box and a gross habit of urohydrosis (grab a Webster dictionary). A pooping mute, what a symbol for my people!

Looking at the mural, Papi comments, "Beautiful. Legend says they are believed to be the ruler of the upper world. They are a symbol of power and health to the people who live in the Andes."

The line is moving at a snail's pace as I look ahead at the crowd of people. We are being herded into two lines: Peruvian Citizens and Non-Citizens. The line for Peruvian citizens is absurdly longer than the Non-Citizens. As me and Papi make our way to the person in the little booth, he asks us "Are jew trabeling for fun or presure? Where are jew stay? Are jew traffic illegal drugs?" (No that last one was fake, but that would be funny!) Papi answers back in perfect English and gets us the stamp of approval.

Reaching the squeaky luggage carousel that a tiny mouse powers with a wheel behind a curtain, Papi stands me in the front and puts our handbags in between my legs. "Don't move and don't take an eye off of our things. I'll be right back."

Grasping our bags for dear life with my toes I look around the airport and "people watch" as I do so often. You can definitely differentiate the American citizens from the Peruvians. The Americans have head to toe designer clothes without being obvious and tote nice luggage. Their shoes look like they just walked out of the sneaker store. They conspicuously flaunt their jewelry and high tech devices. They walk with an air of arrogance as if they are fresh off the catwalk.

Then there are the Peruvians. The closest they've ever been to a runway is at the airport to hose the dust off the planes. The majority of them have worn out clothes that have been passed down from generation to generation so much you can see right through the cloth. They rock a shoe shiner's worst nightmare. The tiredness they wear on their face is the last piece of the ensemble that give their identity away. (Disclaimer, before I get backlash from my very trendy Peruvian cousins who now sport Bebe and Gucci: This was Peru when I lived there in the mid 90's. The Peru of today is quickly transforming into a frightening evolving materialistic consumer-driven country.

Papi comes back with a rusty, half bent, metal rolly cart for our suitcases. After an hour of waiting we finally have all of our worldly possessions on the sickly cart.

We have one final task to overcome as we try to get outside to our eagerly awaiting family. Making yet another line, we walk up to the "Podium of Doom". This is a fairly simple metal podium, on the very top there is one green light and one red light. There is a huge red button on the bottom in the middle. You are supposed to press the button and depending on what color you get you can leave quietly or be stopped and interrogated while your luggage is torn apart by security guards with machine guns. There are old wives tales about the podium. If you press it too hard that means that you are nervous and you are hiding something, RED-LIGHT-STOP. If you press it gently that means that you are in control and have nothing to hide, GREEN-LIGHT-GO.

As we walk up to the podium I start to sweat as the security guards with old western pistols and machine guns glare at me and my fresh kicks. Walking ahead of me I assume Papi is going to do the mandatory button pushing. Just as he gets to the podium he moves out of the way, turns to me and signals for me to press the button. Shaking my head no, I start laughing. I don't want to be the cause of a lengthy, hostile interrogation while a stranger rifles through my panties.

"No, you can do it!" I am holding up the line.

"Go ahead *mamita*." He motions to the podium, putting his trust in my finger.

Looking back at the line of tired faces behind me I muster up the courage to press the intimidating red button. My mind goes blank and I forget the trick! Hard is horrible and gentle is good or hard is handy, gentle is detrimental? Damn my shitty memory! Pressing the big red button "in between" not hard, but not soft. I hold my breath.

… GREEN- GO.

Woo hoo! Papi and I walk out the airport to our motherland, triumphantly, as GREEN-GO'S.

Tira Toffees

Feeling like movie stars, we walk out of the airport to a throng of people waving and shouting for their family members who have just arrived. People who are not passengers are not allowed access to the airport facilities, they have to wait outside. As we walk out I can hear a crowd of people shouting: "Los Yanquis!" For as long as I can remember we were called the Yankees, a colloquial term for anyone from New England (American history, crack open a historically skewed textbook). I am walking into my country of ancestry as a foreigner, a yanqui, a gringa. A Gringa Latina, as Gabriella De Ferrari so eloquently writes (read her book after you put down this one).

As I turn towards the crowd of shouting people, the only person my eyes see is my grandmother. She is standing there with a thin stream of light from the sky beaming down on her despite the dark skies, proud and tall with a smile sent down from the angels. Without a word her thin, white, fragile hands reach out for me and pull me in for a surprisingly strong hug. Breathing in her natural smell and her daily regimen of Jean Nate, I feel safe in her arms. I close my eyes and everything goes quiet around me while I forget for a minute where on earth I am.

Soon I am jolted out of my trance, and I jump around the group of about eleven people, handing out short hugs and kisses.

"Hola. ¿Como estas? Bien... bien. Oh, hola. Tio tia. Ah, si claro." I wear out all my Spanish phrases in those short few minutes.

By the time I get around to everyone I think is part of my family (which is hard to tell) I feel like I completed a short marathon.

"Ay, Adita, you can't wear that outside," Tia Lucy points out, touching my large gold hoop earrings and my skinny gold chain. "Take them off and I will hold them for you until we get home."

I feel naked without my golden armor, but I reluctantly hand over the booty. Making our way to the car my grandmother, Mamita, quietly slips her cold hand into mine, giving me a chill and warmth at the same time.

We immediately get swarmed by a pack of rustic looking men asking to help us with our luggage. These men with ragged clothes and soiled faces are so willing to help us out that I find it incredibly suspicious. My aunts brush them away with polite no's and quick half smiles.

Tia Rosy shovels a handful of change over to a young kid that is keeping an eye on the cars making sure that no one breaks into them. If you don't pay someone to watch your car it is guaranteed you will have a break in. The same kids that look after the cars are the ones that break into the cars of the people who don't pay. They are sure to turn a profit on both ends.

I look out the window as we race down Avenida La Marina, where the streets are lined with palm trees. Sure, it sounds pleasant, but these palm trees are not like the ones you see in Miami. Most palm trees in Lima have been living a dying existence. Growing in garbage-infested gardens and being suffocated by the smog of the city, these palms looked like they are growing in crack-infused soil. These crack palms are pencil thin with brown stringy fronds. Droopy and sad, they are the highlight of the scenery in Lima.

For those of you that are not familiar with Peru or can't even locate it on a map, here is a mini crash course on Peruvian factology. The Republic of Peru is located on the Western part of South America bordered north by Ecuador, south by Chile and Bolivia, east by Colombia and Brazil, and to the west by the Pacific Ocean. (If you still don't have a clue, you must be a product of the American educational system). It is the 19th largest country in the world, approximately three times the size of California (minus all the Mexicans). It is populated by over 23 million people, made up of Whites; European ancestry, Mestizo; mixed European and Indian, Indian; Native American; Afro-Peruvian; from Africa, Asian; China and Japan (Peruvian Chinese food is out of this world ridiculously delicious). The official languages are Spanish and Quechua (I have only met one person in my life that was fluent in the latter, it sounds like Pig Latin). Peruvians are predominantly Roman Catholic (holding on tight to the religion that was forced down their throats by the conquistadors). The official currency is called the Nuevo Sol (named after the Sun God). The average annual family income is $4,400 (bus drivers and mailmen make a little more than $300/month, so don't complain next time you see your paycheck). More than half of Peru is covered in jungle and rainforest including the Amazon (as of right now; if you are reading this 50 years from now, sadly, that might not be accurate). And yes, Peru contributes 75% of the world's production of the cocaine leaf (farmers can earn up to six dollars a kilogram for coca, five times as much as a kilogram of coffee.) Pick your poison.

"So cousin, did you bring any cassette tapes?" My little cousin, Kariqui, questions me while holding up his mammoth walkman with a smile.

"Uh, I have some but I don't know what you listen to, I only have rap... Wu Tang... Nas... Biggie... Arrested Development...."

"You have Coolio, Gangsters Paradise?" he asks in Spanish, curling his C and OO's, making Coolio sound even cheesier than I believe him to be.

Not wanting to hurt his ego about American music, I don't tell him how whack Coolio is with his Pippi Longstocking braids. "Um, I don't think I have that one."

"Really, I can't believe it. What about Kris Kross, Jump Around?" he asks hopefully.

He is really dating himself with that one. "No cousin, I have Tupac in my bag if you want to listen to that one." I grab the cassette tape from my bag.

"Ay ya. Tupac Amaru Shakur! His mother named him after the Peruvian Tupac Amaru el Segundo."

"Who?" I proclaim in bewilderment.

"The infamous Peruvian revolutionary named after the famous Inca? Amaru led an indigenous uprising against the Spanish in the 1800's. His revolt was the first of many by the indigenous people. They cut out his tongue and then they tied his arms and legs to horses. They tried to rip him apart!" Karique shouts flinging his arms and legs out as much as he can in the cramped back seat, pretending he is being quartered. "But he still lived, so they chopped off his head."

Baffled that Tupac's mama named him after a Peruvian, I make a mental note to research that tidbit of info. Tupac, my hero, my poetic lyricist, named at birth after a Peruvian?

"Here listen to this," I offer, handing him *Me Against The World*.

With Mamita's icy hand still in mine I look out the window in silence. The abundance of garbage and dirt makes me feel like we are in a scene from Mad Max. Barbed wire decorates the houses, and with a touch of flair, a line of broken glass encircles the concrete fortresses' outer ledges.

"Are you hungry?" Mamita hands me a toffee she produces out of thin air like a magician. "We can have a little something to eat when we get home," she adds as she squeezes my hand.

Content with my delectable chocolate toffee, it melts in my mouth. As my uncle screeches to a halt at a red light we are rapidly surrounded by a mini-clan of street children. *It is almost midnight, where are their parents?*

"Señora, do you have any change?" one pleads through the slightly open window.

"Señora, please can you help us?" another little one, probably only a little older than Bianca, asks with tears in her eyes.

"Señorita, our mother abandoned us!"

"Poor children," my grandmother murmurs under her breath. Leaning out the window she holds out a handful of toffees to the older one. Leaning forward she grabs the shawl from around her shoulders and gingerly places it on the younger girl's shoulders. "God bless you and may He always be with you," she says as we pull away.

I look back and see a look in the older one's eyes that I will never in my life forget. Not a look of gratitude or appreciation, but a look of pure disappointment mixed with hate. I look out the back window as he tosses the toffees into the cracked street with scorn. *What a little shit!* At the time, all I can see is his ungratefulness for the kindness that my grandmother displayed. I couldn't even begin to see his life and understand how a handful of toffees were not going to bring his mother back, fill his malnourished, empty stomach, or help him save to buy a uniform to attend school.

"Mamita, you cannot give away everything to everyone that asks you for money," Tia Rosy exclaims in exasperation, "You can't save the world."

"Oh... ya... okay... I see," Nodding in agreement while she holds me close and whispers into my ear, "No, not the world, but at least the ones that cross my path."

Singing along with the tape Karique's off tone screeching flows through the car, "When I was sick as a little kid, to keep me hoppy there no limit, to the tings ju did, all my childhood memories, full of all de sweet things ju did for me. And even toe I act craaazy, I gochathank the Lord that ju made me." He croons along, slurring together words like a drunken serenade.

The lyrics remind me of the last conversation I had with my own mom over the phone. Before the phone call, I hadn't seen my mother for almost six months. She disappeared for a while, not returning any of my phone calls. I believe during this time she was probably in her darkest hours both in her marriage and her alcoholism.

Finally, I got in contact with her by chance. "Mami, I have to talk to you," I said into the phone with a lump in my throat. On the verge of tears, I disclose, "Mami, I am moving to Peru with Papi in three weeks."

Waiting for a gasp of surprise or a demand for an explanation as to why, I waited for her response.

"Okay, have a safe trip." Was her cold and non-emotional reply. *CLICK.*

This was not the mother that I grew up with. This cold hearted person was a stranger to me. Even more hurt that I would not be able to say goodbye to my little sister, I threw the phone against the wall. As the phone shattered into pieces, I was immediately sorry that I broke it. Sitting on the nicely carpeted floor trying to put the pieces back together, I began crying and laughing. *I won't need a telephone where we are going anyways.*

"We are home!" Tia Rosy exclaims as we turn left at the big yellow neon sign with a picture of a chicken that reads Pollo Rico. We arrive at 2165 Capac Yupanqui. What a strange name I think to myself, not knowing the history of the great Incan conqueror the street is named after. We stand in front of the lime green door of my grandmother's modest two story light green concrete home. Mashed in between two larger tenements, the house seems to be in hiding. Tia Lucy removes a large metal bar from the front door and proceeds to unlock a series of cryptic locks.

Finally cracking the Da Vinci Code, we step into what would be our home, where I am met by Jesus. *No, not my cousin Jesus.* The first thing you see when you walk into my grandmother's house is a huge antique portrait of Jesus dripping with blood on the cross. Nodding my head as if to say hello, I keep it moving and skate into the living room. My sneakers make a horrible squeaking noise on the freshly waxed wood floors as I take a seat on the stiff couch.

"Let's eat something before you go to sleep." Mamita motions for me to sit at the long dining room table.

Bringing out a variety of small plates and odds and ends, she places a banquet of food on the table: purple olives, fresh cheese, slices of fresh ham, half an avocado, freshly made jelly, a variety of fruits and day old bread from the bakery.

"Just a little bite, before you go to bed." She smiles while munching on an olive.

I gladly dig into the "snack" I am so hungry. As we finish, my aunts and uncles bid their farewells and we are left alone in the light of the bright moon that floods the dining room table. Tia Rosy helps me take my suitcases to my room.

"This is Mamita's room, this is my room, this will be Papi's room, and this will be your room." We walk into a room half the size of my room at home (or what used to be home). The concrete walls are mustard yellow and there is a small yellow twin bed right in the middle. An ancient dresser cowers lonely against a bare wall. The décor is minimalist to say the least.

"Okay, thank you." I want nothing more than to climb into bed and sleep for days.

"I will see you tomorrow," Tia Rosy says, making the sign of the cross on my forehead.

Papi walks in as she is leaving. "You okay?"

"I'm good, just tired."

"Do you need anything?"

My old bed, my old room, my posters on my wall, my old school, my radio stations...my life back?!

"No, I'm fine. Good night Papi."

On my way back from the bathroom I sneak into my grandmother's room. She is sitting on the edge of her bed, with a rosary, quietly praying. Thin and fair skinned, she has soft features and a gentleness about her. Not breaking her mantra, she motions for me to sit next to her with her free hand.

"Padre Nuestro que estás en los cielos... santificado sea tu nombre..."

As she prays she emits an unexplainable energy that makes me feel at peace. She takes away the knot in my stomach that is growing with the uncertainty of what the future holds for me. "Amen." She grabs my hand and gives me the rosary. "Take it, I got it on my journey to Jerusalem. Sleep now, I know you are tired. Dream with the angels." Making the sign of the cross on my forehead, she gives me a bear hug.

"Good night Mamita," I offer, content that she prayed for me at this late hour. "Thank you for praying for me," I add as I walk towards my room.

"Oh my Adelita, you are strong enough to pray for yourself. I was praying for those poor children we met on the street. They are the ones that need help and prayer. Your family is *your* strength," she replies as she slips off her tiny shoes, legs dangling from her bedside.

With the rosary under my pillow, I try to sleep in the ancient, creaky bed, tossing and turning until I am finally able to fall into a deep slumber, with her words echoing in my head: "Your family is *your* strength."

da Vinci in Peru

"GAS! GAS!" The mob screams as they race down the hallways of Conard. I lose my step trying to push my way through the crowd of people and tumble to the ground. The sprinklers go off and in an instant everyone is wet around me. A frail white hand holding a rosary appears through the crowd to help me from the slippery floor as voices scream in my ear, "Cuchios! Cuchios! Cuchios!" Confused and scared, I am ripped from my sleep as I open one eye and find myself in the squeaky bed in the mustard yellow room. Someone in the street is ringing a cowbell and shouting like an auctioneer on speed.

Dragging myself from my lifeless slumber, I raise the metal blinds with a loud clank and peek out to the street below. Through the morning mist I see a little man making a whole lot of ruckus. He is walking down the street, pulling a huge wooden cart behind him with knives hanging from the sides. The array of knives that he carts around clink in a chaotic unison as he screams at the top of his lungs, "Cuchios, Cuchios, Cuchios!" Papi explains to me later that he not only sells knives but he also goes around sharpening old knives to make a living.

An equally small man is walking on the other side of the street in the opposite direction. His wooden cart is almost bare minus a huge metal tank in the middle covered in dirty rags. He sounds like a circus ringmaster, shouting, "GAS! GAS!"

Rubbing the sleep from my eyes, I lay back down. *Toto, I have a feeling we're not in Kansas anymore.* As I pull the blankets up over my head I quickly remember I am far, far away from Connecticut. The humidity in Lima is so high that even the sheets feel wet; not the loveliest feeling when you are trying to get warm.

Kicking the moist sheets from my bare legs I make an attempt to unpack my huge suitcases instead. Opening the tiny closet in my room, I am greeted by the pungent stench of mothballs. As I try to fit my life in my new aromatic closet with prehistoric hangers, I wonder how I ended up here. I begin to think of home and the sting in my stomach I attribute to homesickness gets worse. This is my first day here and I am already thinking about ways I can tell Papi I would like to go back.

"So... when does our flight leave again?"

"Okay... this was nice, really nice. Thanks for the visit."

"Oh... I thought you said do I want to move near the *zoo*!"

Looking at myself in the tiny vanity mirror, I stare back at my sad expression. My pale face, long black hair, and gentle features do not match those of the people in the street, or even those of my family. People would always comment, "Oh, but you don't look Peruvian, you're so pretty!" *Gee, thanks... I think... because I'm pretty sure you just implied that my people are ass-ugly.*

I open a drawer to the vanity to put my tapes away (*Raekwon the purple tape*) and find a pile of old photos. I grab them and replace them with my treasured collection of cassette tapes.

"Where are your shoes? You are going to catch a cold!" Tia Rosy exclaims when I walk downstairs, as if I came down the stairs naked instead of just barefoot. I love sneakers but as soon as I get in the house I kick them off; my feet need to breathe. Shrugging my shoulders, I realize as I open my mouth that I don't have the vocabulary to explain to her, 'Shoes are annoying and I never wear them in the house.' Shoe is zapato or zapatilla? Annoying I have no clue how to say. Casa is house. Trying to piece together my thoughts, I blurt out, "No zapatos para la casa."

"What do you mean? We have to go buy you some shoes then!" Tia Rosy states with concerned surprise.

Solemnly sitting down at the table, I decide not to clarify as I look at Papi for help. He looks on at me in amusement, laughing quietly at the fact that I had just realized that I did not know a lick of Spanish. I *know* Spanish but I don't *speak* Spanish. All those years of replying to Papi in English caught up with me. I understood everything being said, but my thoughts did not magically convert into Spanish as they came out of my mouth. Recall memory is a bitch.

My grandmother comes to the table with a box of General Mills Cheerios in one hand and a can of condensed milk in the other. Placing them before me as if she found the Holy Grail, she announces, "Cheerios! That's what you eat in the mornings, yes?"

Looking at the big yellow box I shake my head in agreement with a smile. Serving my plain Cheerios (not even the honey nut kind) with a splash of heavy, thick condensed milk, I bask in the thought that this is going to be my daily breakfast for years to come: cardboard-like, overly sweet, thick goulash.

"We have Quacker if you want that too," Tia Rosy offers.

"¿Que, Quacker?" I ask.

"Quaker oatmeal," she says in English.

"No I'm okay," I reply, trying not to choke.

On Papi's plate I see the remnants of eggs and toast, and when I meet his eyes across the table he rubs his belly and grins.

"Did you sleep well?" Tia Lucy asks.

I nod my head with a mouth full of dry-yet-soggy Cheerios.

Looking over at Papi, I whisper to him, "I clogged the toilet again can you fix it?"

"Did you put toilet paper in there?" he questions, as if that is the most absurd thing.

"Papi, I forgot!" I say in a loud whisper. It was a normal reflex... wipe then drop. In Peru it is against the law to drop the TP after you pee pee; no, not really but it might as well be. I reason this is because the pipes in Peru are made of cardboard tubes connected by chewing gum. There are little garbage cans everywhere next to the toilets for "proper" disposal. Just the thought of a trash can full of shitty toilet paper makes me nauseous.

"What would you like to eat today?" Mamita asks as I finish my bowl of gummy newspaper, "We can make spaghetti, steak, beans, soup... whatever you want."

"I don't know." I turn to Papi for the million dollar answer.

"She likes lomo saltado, that's her favorite." he remarks as my belly claps for joy.

"Good, then lomito it is!" Tia Rosy exclaims as she clears the table and asks, "Come to the market with me?"

Helping her clear the table, I grab a few plates and bring them to the kitchen, which looks more like a utility closet. There is a prehistoric stove that looks hazardous and a vintage refrigerator to match, outdated countertops, compete with the archaic linoleum flooring. The inside of the refrigerator is as bare as the shelves at the supermarket on the first of the month. The jelly and butter that I put away are the only tenants in their lonely space.

As I turn to go upstairs I notice my grandmother sitting at the kitchen table holding the stack of pictures I brought down from my vanity. She glances at me and holds up a picture of a toddler in a light blue jumper. She gushes, "Your father! Such a good baby then he turned into a rebel! Good-hearted, but always going against the grain. He would argue like his father till the end about equality and equal opportunities for his friends less fortunate."

"Really?" I never really thought about who Papi was before he was my dad.

"Ah and Pepe! How handsome your grandfather was. He is with the other members of the Supreme Court here in Peru in this one," she says handing me the picture. "He was so sweet but my mother did not approve of him at all when he was courting me. Too much of a 'cholo' to even associate with our family. But my 'cholito' proved himself when he became a lawyer and how proud they were when he was appointed to the Supreme Court."

My grandfather, a judge on the Supreme Court? Papi told me stories about him being a lawyer but I had no idea that he served on the Supreme Court. Looking down at a picture of my grandfather with a red and white sash, I see a stranger. He passed away a few months before I was born. The kindness in his eyes jumps out of the picture but I have no memories of him and now I was living in his house.

Mamita comments, "You come from a long line of hard workers and accomplished people. You will keep up the tradition, sweetheart. The Yllanes name is one to be proud of, Adelita."

Not having the vocabulary or the insight into what I would have to accomplish, "Bien" was my meek reply (my grandmother does not know a word of English).

I was supposed to go conquer the world in the name of my family, but first I have to go to the market, because I am famished! My American-Peruvian breakfast concoction left me wanting a big fat breakfast burrito.

Throwing on my semi-baggy jeans and a t-shirt, I stuff my feet into my white Nikes and throw my long hair up into a ponytail. Waiting for Papi, I throw myself onto his bed. His bed is even more ancient than mine, equipped with loose bed springs that stab my side.

"Papi, what's a cholo?"

"A cholo is a person who has mostly Indian ancestry. A person that can trace their blood back to the native people of Peru and not to the white blood of Italy or Spain. Why do you ask?"

"Mamita said that her mom used to call your dad a cholo." I lay still on the bed and stare out the window. "But then Mamita called him a cholo. It's good or bad?"

"Oh, when my grandmother said it, it was bad. You have to remember that my grandmother had light hair with blue eyes! Having my father in the family would taint that pure blood that she held so important, but for Mamita it didn't mean she didn't love my father."

"Funny," I remark, thinking a Peruvian is a Peruvian no matter what their blood looks like.

"Mamita's mother was very prejudiced. She never liked anyone to talk about the fact that the man she married was not of pure blood. My grandfather's great-grandfather was Chinese and a slave! Where do you think you get your straight hair from?"

"Papi, I blow dry my hair straight." I get up from the bed of nails.

As we make our way downstairs we are joined by my Tia Rosy, who looks exactly like Papi only with a wig. She lifts the metal bar from the door that protects us from evil goblins at night, and then she unlocks the series of locks before she lets a flood of sunlight in. The sun tries its best to slash through the everlasting mix of fog and smog that blankets Lima.

Walking towards the market, I am greeted with what people label as "culture shock", though I like to call it the "Mona Lisa Syndrome". The veil of my American existence is quickly ripped from my eyes (and eyebrows). The erratic driving of the taxis, omnibuses, and general public is amplified as we walk just inches away from the high speed chases called daily traffic. The fumes that spill out of the ancient dilapidated vehicles are toxic (rumors are that President Fujimori transported buses from Japan to Peru when they were deemed unfit by their emission standards). Stop signs are only pretty decorations on the side of the road for most.

"Be careful, stay on this side," Papi warns as he shields me from the oncoming traffic and puts himself closer to the street.

We share the tiny cracked "sidewalks" with mounds of garbage and flea infested dogs as we walk along the road. I am an animal lover, anything-with-fur-fanatic. My heart swells when I see a cute dog, but my fascination with dogs quickly turns to disenchantment when I see the number of stray dogs on the streets of Peru. These malnourished, wounded, filthy skeletons of animals are a far cry from the pampered dogs that people in the U.S. carry in their purses. Nuisance or not, I am horrified when my aunt tells me that the government goes around once a year to mass-exterminate these street dogs.

Reading this, one can just imagine the kind of smells that might be produced by this exhaust-emitting, dirty dog filled, polluted street. Multiply that times a hundred and you might begin to imagine how Lima violates your olfactory system. The overstimulation of smells dominates your nose until you don't notice it anymore. The once pungent smell of burnt garbage begins to subside as you walk past the mound of rotting food left on the sidewalk. Everything meshes into one big whiff of nothingness, that is, until you walk by a restaurant or a food stand.

The pleasant smells of Peruvian cuisine make up for all the vile smells that the city produces. Like a peace offering, the aroma of a rotisserie chicken fills the air like a culinary apology. As we walk by the chicken place we see "El Menu" of the day: Papa la Huancaina, Seco, Chicha y Mazamorra Morada. You have your appetizer, main course, drink, and dessert for around 13 soles; about 5 American dollars. As my stomach grumbles, we make our way into the market.

This market is not like those flowery farmers markets we have in the United States. These open air markets are the ones that spring up out of nowhere if you have a beach umbrella and a tomato to sell. I look to the left and see a whole pig, head and all, cooked to a crisp hanging from a butchers hook. To the right I spy a whole uncooked and naked chicken being lynched in a window. Is that what a chicken looks like? I think back to the nice pink drumsticks, vacuum packed with Styrofoam bottoms that I grew up with. *Oh my, chickens have hair?!*

The produce is scattered about and looks odd. I cannot pinpoint what makes these fruits and vegetables look so strange. The lack of conformity within the fruit might be what is throwing me off. You go to Stop & Shop and all the apples are the same color and size. Peppers look perky, shiny, and new. These fruits and vegetables are all unique; some big, some small, different color variations, and none of them look like they belong on the cover of a magazine. *Oh shit, I can't believe it! These are REAL fruits and vegetables! No wax covered genetically altered apples here.*

"Do you want chirimoya?" Papi offers, handing me an ugly looking green fruit that looks like a small, deformed soccer ball.

No! "I guess." I stare back nervously at Miss Piggy and Chicken Little hanging from hooks.

Tia Rosy breaks it open with her hands and exposes the white inside, taking half and biting into it. Hesitant to try the fruit before it is washed, I bite into it and brace for the worst. I envision Snow White biting into the poison apple and falling dramatically to the floor. Quite the opposite, instead I almost fall over with the flavor that floods my mouth. I can't even describe the tastiness that is the fruit Chirimoya. In order to experience it you have to jump on a plane and travel to Peru and snatch one up for yourself. You can find them in your local market but by the time they hit the shelves in the U.S. they have lost their succulent magic.

Slurping my chirimoya, we walk up to the butcher's booth. The butcher wipes his runny nose with the back of his hand as he glances up from a table that looks like a cow was murdered on it.

"Hello, good morning. How are you today, can we have a pound of tenderloin please?" Tia Rosy directs.

Replying with a grunt, he wipes his knife on his apron before slicing into a huge chunk of meat.

"Can you cut it into pieces for lomo saltado, please?" Tia Rosy asks pleasantly.

He begins throwing thinly cut slices onto a piece of newspaper. Swatting away flies, he wipes his brow of the sweat with his forearm. Looking on in amazement at the lack of sanitary conditions, I quietly suffer inside. *Where are your plastic gloves, your hairnet, and your sanitary paraphernalia? You have to wash your hands after you wipe your snot nose! Did you disinfect your knife before you started cutting the meat we are going to eat... with our mouths!?*

I am glad when Tia Rosy finishes buying what she needs, because I'm quickly losing my appetite. Walking back to the house, all I can think about are the filthy conditions of the marketplace, the constant smell of pollution, the garbage that is everywhere except the garbage cans, and the mangy mutts that populate the busy streets. *Shit.* And now, my white kicks are all scuffed up with third world dirt!

These thoughts take over and it is hard for me to focus on anything else…. I feel queasy.

When you have something in your face all the time and don't have anything to compare it to, you don't see it is there (or not there) until you experience something else totally out of your norm. Or until someone points it out to you…

The "Mona Lisa Syndrome", you live in the relative safety of the cocoon the United States weaves for us; you believe this is the absolute truth until you are faced with the complete opposite. What you have been looking at your whole life is not really what you believed it to be. Your everyday reality is not the unconditional truth. Everything jumbles up in your mind when you realize… until someone points out to you… open your eyes! Wake up! Look again for the first time, fool: the truth is, Mona Lisa has no eyebrows!

Piranha Attack

"Yeah, this album is dedicated to all the teachers who told me I'd never amount to nothin'...

all the niggaz in the struggle,

you know what I'm saying.

Uh-ha it's all good baby bay-bee uh!"

With my homeboy Biggie keeping me company, my battery-powered radio playing at a reasonable volume, I finish putting my clothes away in my room. I've been trying to recreate my old room, but I am losing the battle. As I try to stick up my Cappadonna poster, I quickly realize that scotch tape does not adhere to cement walls. Unable to plug in my alarm clock into the deformed outlet without an adapter, I am aggravated after a few minutes. Trying to rearrange my closet, I wonder what tiny hobbit lived here before me. My extensive collection of Air Force Ones and Air Maxes spill out of the closet, forcing me to line my crisp sneakers along the wall.

"Good morning, did you sleep well?" Mamita calmly slips into my chaotically cluttered room. With odds and ends thrown about, she props herself up next to the door.

"Yes I did." I lie, while turning the radio down.

"So many shoes! How many feet do you have?" she jokes, tickling my feet propped on the bed. "Come on let's have breakfast."

She picks up a pile of clothes from the floor and places them on the bed.

Despite the gross-fest that we experienced at the market, the dinner we had the night before was absolutely delectable. I was surprisingly able to devour my lomo saltado; a stir fry of sliced beef, onion, tomatoes and potatoes. My taste buds overloaded as I experienced fresh, unaltered, hormone-free, pesticide-free, free range food. I swore I faintly heard the cow still mooing as I demolished my plate.

As we walk out of the room, I hear Mamita quietly muttering to herself, mimicking a little louder than a whisper, "Niggaz."

Holding back my laughter, shock, and embarrassment, I decide I need to keep my playlist clean from now on. That word does not sit nicely on my grandmother's lips.

The new, oversized house slippers Tia Lucy bought me make loud clunking echoes on the waxed, hardwood floors as I walk down to the dining room. Turning the corner, I bump into a short, dark woman holding a stack of magazines and a dustpan.

"Oh, good morning young lady!" she exclaims brightly.

"Ah, well, hello there," I mumble, giving her a peck on the cheek. She would not be the first stranger I bumped into in the house who just happened to be one of my aunts or cousins.

"Oh." She quickly turns on her heels before I can introduce myself.

As I take a seat at the table, I am dreading my daily dose of Cheerio stew.

"Good morning!" Tia Rosy bends down to kiss my forehead. "What do you want to eat, Cheerios, Quaker, eggs?"

"Eggs." I say quicker than she expected.

"Wouldn't you like a delicious, big bowl of Cheerios instead?" Papi probes as he eats his fried eggs and toast.

Tia Lucy walks in the house a few minutes later, dressed in a dated two piece suit with a small beat up, black briefcase in tow.

"Hello Carmencita! I haven't seen you for a while," she remarks to the small woman I bumped into earlier who has suddenly appeared in the kitchen. "How are the little ones? Have you met my niece Ady yet?"

"Yes, we met earlier." Her eyes fall to the floor.

"Hello," I repeat as I butter my still-hot-from-the-bakery bread.

"Who's that?" I whisper to Papi.

"The housekeeper," he murmurs under his breath.

"They have a housekeeper?!"

"Everyone has a housekeeper here. Even the housekeepers have housekeepers. There is always someone willing to work for what you can afford to pay them here," Papi replies softly.

Recovering from the initial shock of my family having a cleaning lady, I begin to think about the fact that I just kissed the help! Mortified, I hide my face in my plate of scrambled eggs and stuff my face. Let me just tell you that eggs in Peru are in a totally different category than U.S. eggs. Fowl in the U.S. should be ashamed of themselves for dropping such foul eggs!

"What are your plans for today?" Tia Lucy questions Papi.

"Nothing, just going to fix a few things around the house, talk to people about possible jobs, look into Ady's school," he lists while picking up his plate. Mamita swats his arm with the dishrag and takes the plate from his hands.

Oh man! I didn't even realize that this move would consist of me actually attending school. I just finished the school year at

Conard but the school cycles are different in Peru so I would start now and have missed just a few weeks of the start of their school year.

"Can I take Ady to work with me?" Tia Lucy asks Papi.

"If she wants."

I agree with a nod, and excuse myself from the table, "Thank you, *provecho*."

Upstairs I grab jeans and a Nike T-shirt and decide to go with my black Nikes so that they won't get all grimy. As we get outside, we bump into the housekeeper in the tiny front garden. She is tending to the one red rose that occupies the front yard.

"We will see you for lunch Carmencita," Tia Lucy leans in and gives the housekeeper a kiss on the cheek, opens the creaky front gate and we make our way to the street.

So it is okay, to give the help a kiss, I wonder as I walk away confused. After a few steps I look back and see Carmencita gazing on with an equally bewildered look. Nodding my head towards her in recognition, I feel like a dumbass again. I might as well have given her dap, it would have had the same effect. A cloud of rude American-type mentality hovers over me as I walk down the street.

"I don't think I have ever really told you what kind of work I do," Tia Lucy breaks the silence, jolting me out of my thoughts about Carmencita.

"Psychologist, right?"

"No, not really. I have a psychology degree but what I work in is quite different. I work for the government rehabilitating street youth."

"How?" I ask, picturing my aunt sitting with a notepad facing a teen on a long leather couch, talking out their problems.

"You've seen those little yellow and blue stands like that one on the corner? The government runs them and supplies them with goods to sell. The boys that I work with sell at the stands and take home the profit. The majority of the boys that I work with are former *Pirañitas*."

"What's a *Pirañita*?" I ask as we reach the stand at the corner.

A young boy that looks like he is fresh out of diapers walks up to me with a mischievous smile. "A *Pirañita* has no fear. A *Pirañita* is a child who doesn't go hungry at night. A *Pirañita* is a kid who gets what he needs. A *Pirañita* is a man who does what he pleases. *Pirañitas* for life! " He chants before he spits on the ground near my feet and then walks away, knocking over a bucket of dirty water in the process.

"Luis, I told you that if you are going to be working for us you are not allowed to have your brother visit during work. I do not want to see him here again," Tia Lucy scolds the embarrassed little boy behind the stand. He is dressed in a holey sweater with a pair of oversized slacks tied up with a piece of rope. On his feet he dons a pair of tattered, decomposing Skippy's.

"Señora Lucy, I am sorry, I won't let it happen again. I really didn't know that he was going to come here. I promise, I am doing better please don't be mad," he pleads.

"I am keeping an eye on you Luis. I will be back at the end of the day. Do you need anything?"

"No, I have everything. Thank you Señora Lucy," he says gratefully, giving her a hug.

Walking towards the next booth Tia Lucy elaborates, "The *Pirañitas* is a child street gang here in Lima. A lot of the members do not have parents, some are runaways. Luis is lucky enough to have a mother but she is cripple."

"Oh yeah? We have gangs in Connecticut too. Are these little kids in danger?"

"The only danger they have is the police. The police can kill these kids and have no one to answer to. These kids need money and they try to get it any way possible. They rob, steal, and cheat for their survival. They eat according to what they steal. That is why they call them the *Pirañitas*."

Never having heard the word before, I question, "What is *Pirañitas*?"

"I am not sure the word in English but the little flesh eating fish that swarm and attack to eat their prey?"

"Oh piranha, *Pirañitas*, little piranhas," I muse, my mind filled with a mental picture of a piranha attack.

"If they catch you walking the streets alone they attack and swarm... like piranhas. They are ruthless."

Walking up a few blocks we pass the *Banco de la Nación* where there is an armed guard protecting the outdoor ATM. Wearing a brown uniform and military boots he is strapped with a huge machine gun and a machete clipped to his leg. This is a far cry from the fat sloppy guards we have in Bank of America armed with long plastic flashlights and lollipops. I'm trying not to stare at the assassin in brown, but he is obviously grilling me as we walk past. He is giving me that undressing you with his eyes stare.

His improper looks are nothing new. It seems like the men in Lima are sex deprived, because every time I walk outside I am greeted with their hungry looks. The *"piropos"* (catcalls) are far from creative and seem to be straight up disrespectful. Truth be told, on top of it all these men are extremely unattractive. I can honestly say that to me, Peruvian men are not attractive at all. In all my life, I have never seen a stunning Peruvian male (sorry, Benjamin Bratt, you're easy on the eyes but not handsome). Maybe only women are allowed to swim in the good looking gene pool, because all of my female cousins are drop dead gorgeous.

Reaching the next candy shack we are greeted by a cute little kid whose eyes gleam when he sees Tia Lucy.

"Hello Señora Lucy! How are you today?" He looks like he is about seven years old.

Giving Tia Lucy a lingering hug he grabs my outstretched hand and pulls me in for a peck on the cheek. He smells of Old Spice, but you can still tell that he has not washed his clothes in a very long time.

"This is my niece Ady, she just moved here from close to *Nueva York*. Ady this is Rodolfo, he is one of my best workers."

"Hello... nice to see you, here, at work, nice day" I drag out awkwardly not knowing what else to say.

"Rodolfo do you mind keeping her company for a few minutes? I have to go run into the *Chinos* to pick up some pic...." It sounds like a request, but Tia Lucy is walking away before she even finishes her sentence.

You could say that I am somewhat uncomfortable standing there with an ex-criminal watching over me in a place unfamiliar to me. I picture this little thing of a boy clocking me over the head and robbing me, but I glance down and realize that I have nothing to steal anyways. I left all my jewelry at home, and with empty pockets I feel relieved. As the time ticks slowly, Rodolfo reaches overhead from where he's sitting in his shack, and slowly pulls out a shiny object from over his head. As if in slow motion, I see it before it registers in my brain; a silver glistening gun! Oh shit, damn it, I knew it!

"Sublime?" He offers handing me a square piece of chocolate wrapped in shiny silver paper.

"Ah... okay... thank you," I stutter, embarrassed that I believed he would rob me for my Nikes.

"Nike?"

His question surprises me, "What?"

Pointing to his own shirt and then to mine, he repeats, "Nike, you like Nike?" He pronounces Nike as if it rhymed with bike. It's only when I look down that I remember I am wearing a Nike t-shirt. My gaze shifts to look at his obvious bootleg t-shirt, which has a crooked looking Nike swoosh logo that is also pointing in the wrong direction and shoulders that have the three white stripes from the Adidas logo.

"Yeah, I like Nike." I make sure to rhyme Nike with bike, to not point out his obvious error in name brands. "Thanks for the chocolate." I savor the last bite of real cacao and bona fide milk heaven.

After an awkward silence I ask him how long he has been working with my aunt.

"Little over a year, Señora Lucy bumped into me in the center of Lima. Asked her for change, she told me about these stands. Said I could make up to two dollars a day depending on how good I was. Didn't have other plans so came here to Lince. Make enough here so I can go back home in few years."

Not sure what reply is appropriate in this situation, I draw a blank and stay quiet with a silly grin on my face instead. Trying to keep away from a stray dog that is looking at me for a bit of chocolate, I walk in a semicircle in front of the shack. My aunt warned me about catching fleas from the street dogs and transporting them into the house.

"All set. Now we go to the market to get food for lunch." Tia Lucy remarks as she walks out of the photo shop to rejoin me. I bid farewell to Rodolfo, glad that I am literally not in his hole-infested Skippy shoes.

"He was nice," I comment.

"Oh he is a great kid. I wish I could take him in and take care of him but there are too many children that need help. Rodolfo was scared and confused when I met him. I was in the Center of Lima doing some errands when he tried to steal my purse! He wasn't very good at it. He fell to the floor when the rope I had wrapped around my purse snapped him back. I told him that I would buy him lunch if he apologized for trying to rob me. We spoke and he told me that he ran away from home because he felt guilty that his mother had to feed him. Some days she would have to choose between feeding him or his baby sister so he ran away so his sister wouldn't starve."

"He was wandering Lima alone?"

"No, the *Pirañitas* picked him up. They taught him how to beg for change, how to fake tears, and how to clean windshields to make money. Unfortunately, they also showed him how to get high."

"High from what?" I imagine Rodolfo and his crew smoking a diesel blunt of weed.

"Everything. They sniff whatever they can get their hands on: glue, paint, tar. It kills their brain, makes them change." She shakes her head. "I have seen too many kids who never come back from that."

Rodolfo made Oliver twist look like Richie Rich. When I was seven I was collecting and trading Garbage Pail kids. My mornings were a busy schedule of Inspector Gadget, Smurfs, Transformers, and Punky Brewster. I never had a second thought about where my next meal was going to come from. My tummy has never been abused.

As we turn the corner we walk past a playground or "play-around". This park-o-fun is equipped with a wobbly seesaw and a painfully uncomfortable looking metal slide. The ground is barren; just a plot of dirt that must have seemed like a good place to plop a playground. Two girls inside are playing with an old bike tire kicking up clouds of dirt, and there are four dangling chains where there should have been a seat for a swing.

A country of thieves. People are working with the bare minimum and no one seems to have any to spare. There is always the constant fear that someone is going to rob you, your car, or your house. The lack of trust among your fellow countrymen is apparent. Maybe this constant paranoia was passed down from generation to generation since the era when the Spaniards came and stole riches from our land. While they pillaged the silver and gold, they also stripped the Peruvians of their trust. This was encoded in their DNA. "Trust no one!" Even the trees in Lima look bare. Steal the leaves right off the trees to use them for napkins at the dinner table (we *are* resourceful).

We stop by the corner market, and I walk through with my eyes half closed. Tia Lucy grabs all the ingredients she needs, and we make our way back home. We deposit our two tiny bags of groceries into Mamita's kitchen and by the time we make our way back downstairs to the dining room, it magically transforms into a delicious lunch. That's when I find out we also have a hired cook that comes in twice a week.

"Ady this is my friend, Marujita. She is from the church." Mamita gestures towards a tiny, elderly woman sitting at the table with a fork and knife already in each hand. She has tucked her napkin into the top of her shirt like a bib.

"Hello," I greet her.

Mumbling, the little hunchbacked visitor smiles and reveals her lack of teeth. How on earth is she going to eat the steak, I wonder? She would only be the first of many random guests that my grandmother invited to eat with us. She happily slurps her steak away in a content silence.

After finishing our lunch we all make our way upstairs and I gladly make my way to take a daily siesta. But opening the door to my room, I am shocked at all the clothes I have still thrown about. I notice the abundance of clothing I possess and think about Rodolfo and the other boys that work in the shacks. They probably make in one year what I spend on one pair of sneakers.

Grabbing a tissue I blow my nose and to my horror I see that my boogers are black! If you have ever experienced this, most likely, you have traveled to a third world country (or live in Jersey). The constant respiration of city pollution wreaks havoc on your nose hairs trying to filter out the poison. Curling up on top of the pile of clothes I bury my head into the mountain of retail and close my eyes. As I drift off, I have dreams of piranhas attacking my closet.

Pacharmaanica

Pachamama, Mother Earth- or literally translated, Mother World- is a goddess worshiped by the Andean people. This deity is said to be the goddess of fertility who presides over planting and harvesting. You are to spill a small amount of chicha (a fermented Peruvian drink… people from the Caribbean, please refrain from giggling; ask a Puerto Rican what chichar means) on the ground in her honor. When you fail to do so she gets angry and her disapproval is the scientific explanation for earthquakes.

If you have never experienced an earthquake before you can compare it to a hangover. Everything is shifting and moving while you are standing perfectly still. I open my eyes and even though it is pitch black, I know that something is not right. I sit up just as my door flings open.

"Ady, come, you have to move!" Tia Rosy shrieks as she runs towards my grandmother's bedroom.

Springing from my bed, I hurry to stand next to my closet as picture frames and books fall from the shelves and crash to the ground. Frozen with fear, I can't move my feet, they have turned to cinder blocks.

"Mama, come stand here." Papi motions for me to stand in the doorframe of my room.

What the hell is the doorframe going to do for me if the walls come crashing down? Wouldn't it be safer in the basement? Oh, I forgot we don't have a basement; no one in Lima does. I have no idea why this is; please write to me if you have a reasonable explanation.

Cowering on the floor in the doorframe with my hands covering my head, I look across the hallway for my grandmother. With baby pink rollers in her hair and a cool smile on her lips, she stands under her doorframe in her half open night robe and waves to me as if nothing out of the ordinary is happening. As quickly as it came, the trembling stops.

"*Pucha madre that* was a big one!" Tia Rosy proclaims as she walks around, picking up the fallen casualties of the earthshake.

"Everyone safe? Calm, *ya*, I'm going back to sleep then," Mamita chimes in. She loves sleep as much as I do. I inherited the siesta gene from her.

Legs shaking, I climb into my bed as Papi follows, "Are you okay? I forgot to mention earthquakes."

"Yeah, ya did, but I'm fine." In fact, I am scared shitless. There are absolutely no earthquakes in Connecticut. Snow storms, thunder storms, hurricanes, hail storms, and maybe tornado "watches", but never, "going to demolish the structural foundation of your home" earthquakes.

Papi fixes the blankets and folds them nicely on top of me, "Try to go back to sleep."

I close my eyes and stay awake until the maniac with the knives strolls down our street. In place of an alarm clock now I have a small dirty man shrieking, "Cuchios, cuchios, cuchios!" to wake me from my slumber every morning.

Wide awake already, I decide to go downstairs, where I catch a glimpse of a crisp white envelope on the floor underneath the mail slot. I open the letter addressed to a Miss Adeline Yllanes, 2165 Capac Yupanqui, Lima 14 PERU. The word PERU is written bigger than the rest of the words and underlined with a big black marker (not to be confused with the 2165 Capac Yupanqui, Lima, United States).

Taking a seat on the hard ass Flintstones couch in the living room, I read my mother's nicely placed cursive writing. Her penmanship is so beautiful it is a shame to waste it on such harsh words.

Ady,

I hope you having wonderful time in Peru and you get to know your granma. She is a gret beutiful person. I wish you all the best in your new life but I just want to tell you I will no longer be a part of your life. I am doing gret here withoud you and I belive you and you father are doing just fine withoud me. I hope you unerstant and wish you the bess in your future life. Please do not try to contact me as we have moved.

Sincerely,

Your mother Anna

I flip the letter over as if looking for more; an explanation, or maybe even the words "Just Kidding!!!" written on the back. Confused and angry, I struggle to hold back the flood of emotions rising up from my belly. The lump in my throat gets bigger as I re-read the letter. What did I do? I had been writing my mother letters on the regular. I sent letters to my sister at summer camp complete with stickers and hearts. Mami never replied but Chiara wrote back often.

Tia Rosy came downstairs and found me staring out the window trying to keep the tears in.

As she sits beside me, she fills in the silence, "Good morning sweetheart. Did you sleep well?"

Nodding my head yes, hot tears run down my face as Tia Rosy picks up Mami's letter from the floor. Without a word she places me in her arms and lets me cry. For a while we just sit there as I wail like a sad puppy abandoned by her mother.

Probably having seen the name on the envelope, after a while she speaks about my mother.

"You know I was friends with your mama first. Your Tia Lucy use to date your Tio Rolando. Your mother and I became good friends; she would always be at our house. She had such a close relationship with Mamita. One day your father noticed her for the first time. Your mother is a good person; she just had a hard childhood. I don't know if you know about it and she should be the one to tell you more but just understand she was bounced around a lot from family to family when she was very young. She does not deal with her emotions like one would expect."

Calming down enough to hear her story, I am still not yet ready to divulge any information. This must have been a mistake. Trying to rationalize the letter in my head, I realize that she must have written it when she was under the influence. She was always so emotional when she drank and made very poor choices.

"Do you think I can call her after breakfast?" I wipe the salty tears from my cheeks.

"Of course, let's get breakfast on the table before your father comes down," she suggests as she walks to the kitchen.

Having lost my appetite, I hardly pay attention to the morning conversation.

"Right mama?" Papi's question breaks into my thoughts, and I glance up to see him looking to me for a reply.

"Hum, what?" I say in a flat tone, still not focused.

"You are never going to marry and take care of me when I get old," he jokes.

"I don't know," I say with a shrug of my shoulders, never thinking that Papi could grow old. *He is my Peter Pan, my forever young, my knight in shining armor.*

"Tia Maruja was the first girl, she was the one that was supposed to not get married and take care of Mamita instead. In times past, the first born daughter was designated to take care of the elderly parents and dedicate their life only to them. Not like old people in the United States, they get sentenced to life in nursing homes!" Tia Rosy proclaimed, knowing firsthand about American life since she went to high school in Kentucky for a year when she was a teenager.

"You put a nursing home here in Lima and you will go out of business," Papi offers.

"Oh, I can take care of myself, *you* just don't want to live by yourself." Mamita says to Tia Rosy. "Come on, let us get ready, I have to stop by the market to buy a few items for the Pachamanca tonight."

"Pacha-who-ca?" I interrogate Papi.

"Paaa-chaaa-maaa-ncaaa! You'll see."

Already mentally preparing to visit the snotty, smelly butcher I am pleasantly surprised when Mamita says we are going to a market on the other side of town. Since we walk everywhere, take a taxi, or a mini-bus (omnibus), we hardly ever make use of the car in the garage. Like a prisoner, the fairly new car is enclosed with lock and key... and chains... and iron bars. It takes a while to take the car out of the fortress, but the car finally rolls out looking like a Mercedes Benz compared to the other clunkers on the road. Tio Lucho, being a successful brain surgeon in Spain, was able to buy Mamita her modest house and reliable Nissan Sentra.

"You going to drive?" Papi questions Tia Rosy.

"Of course."

"Okay if you say so, I didn't know Peruvian women knew how to drive," he jokes with his younger sister.

"Just hush up and get your bones in the car," she demands.

"Tia Rosy used to steal our father's car when she was only about eight years old. She would have to sit on top of phone books and Bibles to see above the dashboard. It was sacrilegious," Papi whispers to me as Tia Rosy slips into the driver's seat.

Crossing the main road, Javier Prado, my knuckles turn red as I squeeze the door handle. I feel like I am in a bumper car as we narrowly dodge other vehicles. Tia Rosy uses her horn every time she takes a breath, and her turn signals probably have cobwebs on them.

We pull up to a clean white sign with red letters, marking what would be the very first time I step into the supermarket **E WONG**. A young guy in a striped white and red shirt comes to Tia Rosy's side of the car as she steps out. *Valet parking?!* I hear angels sing as I step into the aisles of the orderly, sanitized, odorless super haven.

"I just have to get a few things but if you see anything you want put it in the shopping cart." Mamita remarks, nodding her head in the direction of the chocolate section.

There is every kind of chocolate imaginable (minus any typical American brands). I fog up the glass as I eye all the handmade chocolates in a display case.

"Can I help you? These... right here... with filling... special... every... think." a pretty young girl says as she pops out from behind the display case wearing a short red and white uniformed dress. I catch the first part of what she's saying but she's talking so fast that I can only grasp half of what she is trying to sell me. Not only is she talking super-fast but she is not pronouncing all the syllables and she is using slang not familiar to me.

"No, I okay," I respond awkwardly as I turn to walk away.

"Here," she says, handing me a small chocolate on a white napkin with a sympathetic look.

"Thank you... for the chocolates," I mumble, walking as fast as I can in the other direction. She probably thinks I'm retarded, sorry... mentally challenged.

I walk down the aisles in amazement. The setup is much like grocery stores back home where most of the items are packed up nicely in the sanitary manner that I am used to. Walking towards the aroma of freshly baked bread, I find a corner with bread in all shapes and sizes: sweet bread, sour bread, croissants, rolls, Portuguese bread, bread filled with chocolate, every bread imaginable, except for sliced bread. Why have plain pre-packaged sliced bread when you could have fresh bread every day? The only sliced bread that is sold in Peru is by a brand named BIMBO. So scandalous, I always giggle when I see it.

I nod in approval as I walk by the meat department; no funky smell, no flies, no sweaty butcher behind the counter. All the meat is vacuum packed in plastic and Styrofoam, like it is in nature. The butcher stands behind the counter ready to help customers with a clean white jacket and equally clean starched white hat that stands erect on his head.

I bump into Papi as I turn the corner. "Oh, Papi I like this place!"

"Did you want something?"

"Yeah, everything, but nothing in particular. What does Wong mean? It sounds Chinese." I resist my urge to dump everything into the cart.

"This chain was started by a family of Chinese immigrants that came to Peru. They opened their first store in the forties."

"This place is huge... and clean."

Meeting up with Mamita and Tia Rosy, I hide my face as we walk by the chocolate display case. Grabbing a delicious looking cherimoya right before check out, I place it gingerly into the cart. Content with my new-found discovery, I smile as we pass the sign, **WONG donde comprar es un placer**... (yes indeed!)

We reach Tia Lilly's house in the upscale neighborhood of Miraflores. Driving as if she were on the Audubon, Tia Rosy weaves in and out of the ridiculous traffic to the other side of the tracks where actual flowers are in bloom in the parks; no robbing of shrubbery here. We pass a huge structure that looms over the apartment buildings called Huaca Pucllana, a pre-Incan temple towering above the middle of a busy intersection.

While passing a park with rows and rows of ancient looking trees, Tia Rosy points out, "This is Parque de los Olivos. You see that tree? That tree was brought over on the boat to Peru by Pizzaro himself. And this school here on your right is Maria Reina where you will be attending."

"Oh yeah?" The school looks like a fortress. It is enclosed with a high wall and all I can see is a uniformed man sitting atop a corner from a lookout perch.

As we reach Tia Lilly's house, I ask if I can call my mother.

Papi and I walk to the corner to a tiny shop supplied with three computers and a line of booths with pay phones. Making our way to the attendant Papi turns to me and asks, "How long are you going to be talking for?"

"I have no clue. Why?"

"I have to buy tokens for every three minutes you talk, so I have to know how many to buy." He responds, trying to explain the process of making a long distance phone call in a third world situation.

"I guess not that long, maybe five minutes?" *I also suck at math.*

After paying the attendant we make our way into an eerie looking Doctor Who phone booth. Picking up the receiver, Papi dials Mami's number. (If you are still stuck on the Doctor Who phone booth phrase Google -It). Holding my breath, I am afraid I won't know what to say when she answers. Feeling dizzy as I hold my breath for the ridiculously long series of numbers, 011-511-860-463-0649, I finally get a faint ringing on the other end.

Papi goes outside to smoke as I stare out the window, the phone rings and rings. Through the buzzing and static I hear a woman's voice.

"Mami? Hi, it's Ady! Mami?" I shout.

"We're sorry you have reached a number that has been disconnected or is no longer in service..." The female voice with a British accent repeats over and over.

Feeling a sinking in my stomach, I whisper into the phone, "Oh hello, Mami it's me. I was just calling to tell you I love you and I miss you. I just wanted to hear your voice." CLICK.

"How is your mother?" Papi asks as I step outside with my jaw clenched and fists tight.

"Fine."

POOF... and that was the end of Mami for a few years, until the accident and the cheerful, cumbersome fat guy that brought her back to life (no, not Santa Claus).

Walking back to Tia Lilly's house, I try not to carry Mami's decision with me.

"Welcome! Hello how are ju?" Tia Lilly greets me in English. "Very nice to see ju. My name is Lilly Yllanes Monge. Where is dee restroom?" she jokes, converting back to Spanish to add, "And that is all I know how to say in English my love!"

Always the jokester of the family, Tia Lilly looks like a younger version of Mamita. She is tall and slender with beautiful green eyes. Her husband is a short, equally comical but refined gentleman. Greeting the droves of relatives inside, I introduce myself to cousins and uncles I have never met before now. I'm semi-exhausted by the time Tia Lilly drags me to the back of the house. The surrounding buildings create a mini fortress that encloses the backyard with concrete, bricks, and clothes lines. I smile at a neighbor that is peering over his balcony onto the party that is forming down below.

"Here is the Pachamanca!" Tia Lilly exclaims unveiling a hole in the ground.

"Oh, nice!" I say as if I were a Pachamanca expert.

Looking at my reaction as if there is no need to explain, she enters the kitchen. "Come you can help, I started already early this morning but you can help setting everything up."

There are huge pots on the ancient stove filled with everything imaginable. Taking Tia Lilly's lead, I help haul out big steel pots to the backyard.

We must be having a barbeque, I think as we grab the last of the food. But when I scan the backyard for a grill, I see none.

Instead, Papi is gathered around the hole in the ground along with my other uncles and cousins trying to contain a small fire.

"You see, I had to invent this apparatus because the rocks here in Lima are pieces of shit compared to the rocks in Huancayo." Tio Pepe growls as he brings out a strange metal contraption. It looks like one of those big metal cage looking things that women used under their dresses in the 1800's. Getting a fire going, the whole family gathers in a circle as everyone starts placing the food on top of the fire pit. The metal device is placed on top and then banana leaves are quickly woven into the grooves. After making a big mound of food and stones, it is then covered by a burlap bag and dirt is thrown upon it along with chunks of grass. Patting down the big mound of food and earth with a shovel, Papi looks like a little kid again. With a big smile, he stands atop the mountain of mash.

Having never even heard the word Pachamanca before I am not mentally prepared for the fact that we are going to be eating food covered in dirt. As unappetizing as it seems to me, everyone else seems to be mesmerized by the fact that we are having a Pacharmaanica, or whatever it is called.

"Here Ady, you are the guest so you can place the cross." Tia Rosy calls out to me from across the mound, holding out a cross made out of a palm leaf.

Placing the cross on the top of the Pachamanca to bless the food, I pose for a picture. **CLICK**. Buen provecho!

Despite the fact that I am starving I have no idea how I am going to sit there and wipe dirt off my chicken before I eat it. Would I have to floss the grass out of my teeth after we eat? I ask Papi when I can look forward to the dirt-fest.

"Four hours."

Four hours, are we cooking our food with tiny matches?! Crap, I am hungry now. Eyeing a bowl of something unfamiliar on the table I take a handful of what looks like monster unpopped popcorn.

"Papi gross, what is wrong with the popcorn?"

"That's not popcorn, mama, that's cancha."

The salty dryness hits my mouth like a wave of sand. I finish the tiny balls of sandpaper and decide not to grab another handful.

"Here Ady, hold her for a minute, I have to grab the corn." Tia Lilly hands me a small baby wrapped in a soft, pink blanket.

I assume I am holding one of my baby cousins because we never got formally introduced. I am still in awe about the number of relatives that I have in Peru. My family tree is more like a family forest. Making my way to the Pachamanca, I walk around it with curiosity. With the baby in my arms, I sit down next to it on a nice patch of grass to stretch my legs.

As soon as I sit down it seems like the whole party comes to a halt. It is dead quiet as everyone turns at the same time to look at me.

Papi jumps up from the table with a stick in his hand. Walking quickly towards me he holds the stick in the air as if he is coming towards me to stab a vampire in the heart. Flinching, I close my eyes as he impales the ground next to me with the stake.

"Papi!" I squeal.

"You don't have to believe, but you have to abide," he says holding his hands up as if to say everything is under control. Taking a seat next to me on the ground he continues, "It's just a superstition but you are to never place a new baby on the bare ground. It is believed that if you do... Pachamama will call them back to the Earth."

I envision a tiny baby casket being lowered to a hole in the ground.

"Oh my!" I exclaimed, quickly getting up from the floor. I don't want to be the cause of a baby's death, I just wanted to stretch my damn legs.

"If you stick a branch or knife into the ground this protects the baby from any harm."

Embarrassed, I hand the baby to Tia Rosy. Making my way into the kitchen I find a big pitcher of Chicha with chunks of fresh pineapples floating in it. I quench my thirst with two big glasses of the deliciousness. Who would have thought that purple corn would taste good enough to drink? Drinking too quickly, a small stream drips down the side of my mouth and falls to the earth. No earthquakes today.

After a few hours of munching and chit chatting in my slowly growing elementary Spanish vocabulary, it is time to unveil the Pachamanca. My grandmother stands over the mound and recites a ridiculously long prayer as we all wait in silence. Stomachs growling, the men soon gather around and unearth the food.

Sitting at a small wooden table I look around for plates and utensils. I look and notice everyone is tearing up the food with their hands and eating straight off of the banana leaves. Papi places a little bit of everything at the table in front of me and I gladly dig into the little packages. The first bundle is a bit of chicken. This chicken is so tasty I am sorry I ever thought that KFC was real chicken. *This* is finger lickin' good. I have the freshest tasting pork I ever laid lips on. The corn is so big, sweet and fresh I eat five ears. The potatoes are complete with a little

Aji (a mixture of hot peppers, parsley, onions and slices of heaven). Licking my fingers to the bone, I indulge in one of the best meals I ever had in my life.

Stomach full and content all I can say turning to my father as I rub my belly is, *"Paaa-chaaa-maaan-caaa!"*

Inti

Inti, the Sun God, is the patron deity of Tahuantinsuyo. The Incan Empire was divided into four sectors, together known as Tahuantinsuyo. The four regions met at the capital of Cuzco where Inti blessed my people with his presence. (Okay, okay, technically not my people because I cannot trace my ancestry back to the Incas, but you cannot deny the connection that all Peruvians have with the Inca people no matter the actuality that their blood reveals). Tahuantinsuyo… Tahuantinsuyo… the name itself paints a civilization of strength, knowledge, and power. Inti, the sun, was the most important aspect of their lives because it provided them with warmth and light. Inti was the giver of life. On the surface, Inti was a tangible power, but if you let your mind wander a bit into the realm of mysticism that surrounds the Incas, you can take Inti to be something more profound. Quite literally, if you are fluent in English and Spanish, IN-TI, means IN-YOU. The giver of life, the provider of everything that is needed to survive and be a great entity, is IN-YOU, not in the sun. Stuck in a place between English and Spanish, I had to discover the warmth of Inti… in me.

The warmth inside of me at the moment is freezing in the shower. Here, an hour before you want to take a hot shower you have to flip a Frankenstein-looking lever in order to warm up the bucket of water on the roof that then provides you with a spit worth of warm water. A far cry from my half hour long scalding-hot showers I am accustomed to taking, these early morning dunk-in-a-warm-stream-of-piss-water-sessions are unbearable. Soon after washing my body I would have to scramble to wash my long hair in a race against time, and by the time I rinse out the conditioner from my long hair, the water is ice cold.

Curious about where they store the hot water, I venture up to the roof of my grandmother's house. When I climb the concrete spiral staircase, I spot an ancient water heater that looks like the little engine that could. Peering over the ledge of our two story abode I have a beautiful view of grimy Lima. The smog rivals Los Angeles and the crumbling buildings compete with those of Cuba for the title of 'most dilapidated'. Lima is a panorama of poverty. *What did I get myself into?*

"Don't sit there with your wet hair *princesina, te va dar 'aire'*," Tia Rosy urges as I head back downstairs to sit at the head of the table next to the doorway for lunch.

Ever since I got to Peru people have been talking about *"aire"*. I never seen it and I imagine it is a deadly thing if you ever do run into it. Something akin to a breeze, it seems to be much more sinister and deadly. *Aire* is the cause of all things unexplainable. You are forbidden to move from a hot spot to a cold spot without easing into it first. Forget about doing cannonballs into a pool, you have to make a slow transition to not catch the *"aire"*. The medical diagnosis for catching pneumonia, flu, colds, and paralysis is simply *"aire"*.

Completely ridiculous! I will not let these superstitious beliefs persuade me into changing my daily routines, I reflect as I slowly change my seat to a less drafty spot. What a crock of shit, I think, as I carefully wrap a sweater around my shoulders.

"Mamita, do you need help?" I call from the table, not hearing the usual clanking of pots yet.

She walks out from the kitchen in her Sunday best despite it being a weekday. "Rosy didn't tell you my love? We are going out to eat for lunch. Tia Lucy is going to meet us."

I bolt to my room so we can hurry up and eat, my belly needs grub! I quickly dry my hair with a blow dryer so no one will have a heart attack as I step outside. Even though we are in the mid-winter months it is still super warm to me. The temperature is constantly in the mid 60's. I'll take this cold winter over a Connecticut winter any day. I don't particularly like the North-Eastern so-cold-it-hurts-when-you-breathe winters.

Outside it is warm but overcast, I feel like I am walking through a Steven King novel. The light mist that blankets the sidewalk is gloomy and doesn't help my mood very much. I am quietly suffering from homesickness and the upcoming D-Day for starting school is not helping.

One third of the Peruvian population lives in the metropolitan district of Lima. Imagine 7 million people squeezing into Rhode Island. I don't think Rhode Islanders would approve of this kind of invasion, but just imagine it. As we hit the main street in Lince the taxi we hailed is suddenly surrounded by a swarm of people selling Chiclets, bananas, cigarettes, Tupperware, pirated VHS's, books, and even toilet seats.

"Do you want to snack on some chips?" Tia Rosy offers looking at an old woman with chips in one hand a toilet seat in the other.

"No thanks, I'm not that hungry," I lie, even though my stomach is eating itself.

The taxi driver almost runs over the vendors that are at our sides. We soon pull up to a very dazzling, very bright, yellow and orange establishment. The huge neon blue sign reads BEMBOS, it looks like a fast food joint.

Noticing my face, my father remarks, "You're American, they think you are made of burgers and fries."

We got all dressed up to go to an equivalent of a McDonalds? (Which, by the way, are almost nonexistent here.) Walking into the establishment it is surprisingly very bright and clean, and the sanitary environment instantly puts my mind at ease. Since

I'm still getting tongue tied when I speak Spanish, I let Papi order for me. The very young attendant in uniform speaks to Papi so fast I don't catch more than half of the exchange.

We sit down to out-of-this-world monstrous burgers. Now when I say burger, you are probably visualizing the traditional rock hard round slab of frozen cow meat that eventually crawls its way to a bland, thin bun you get from McDonalds. What we are eating shouldn't even be called a burger, it should be re-named a superb-urger! The meat is a mouthful of spices so amazing that it would be a crime to cover the zest with any sort of condiments. The meat is only one component in the savory superb-urger; the bun is equally delectable. It tastes like it just jumped from the oven to my plate. Unlike a regular bun, it seems to have a hint of sweetness that embraces the meat in a lovely dance.

"Do you like your burger?" Tia Lucy questions, interrupting my love affair with my food.

"Yeah," I reply curtly, wanting my mouth to do nothing more than eat at this point.

Pausing for a moment, I notice everyone is holding their burgers using the foil that the burger is wrapped in as if not to touch the actual burger. These are also the same people that eat pizza with forks and knives. Having grown up eating with my hands, I probably looked like an uncivilized cavewoman. Chicken wings, pizza, burgers, sandwiches... finger foods. Mashed potatoes, spaghetti, soup, and ice cream... not finger foods.

"These fries are unbelievable." I turn to Papi with stars in my eyes.

"*Yuquitas*, yucca fries," he says in between bites. He opted to eat his burger with his bare hands like me.

"Drinking cold Inca!?" Tia Rosy asks, sounding surprised. "You are going to get sick for sure," She adds as she stabs a *yuquita* with her fork. Refrigerated drinks are okay in the summer but strictly ludicrous in the winter.

The Inca she is referring to is the Inca Kola that is served in every establishment in Peru. Named the "Golden Kola" for its golden hue, at first glance one might think it tastes like pineapple or bananas. Far from it, I think it tastes like bubble gum. A large number of people believe that the main ingredient, *hierba luisa*, is medicinal. When you say Inca Kola to any Peruvian living in Peru or abroad you bring to them a feeling of pride. It conjures up images of ceviche, Machu Picchu, humitas, mazamorra morada, tumis, and Incas. Slogans include "Peru's Drink" (*La Bebida del Perú*),"Made of National Flavor!" (*¡De Sabor Nacional!*), and the latest, "The flavor of Peru" (*El Sabor del Perú*). Well in actuality, Inca Kola, the national drink and the symbol of Peruvian pride was created by none other than an Englishman. Juan R Lindley is *really Joseph R. Lindley* hailing from jolly ole' England! Joseph started the production of Inca Kola as an immigrant to Peru in 1910. This is tantamount to Americans finding out that Betsy Ross was a Mexican (please visit your local library if you have no idea what Betsy Ross accomplished).

"You are not hungry?" I ask Mamita, as I pick at her yucca fries. (It is **not** pronounced yuck-a, repeat after me... you-ca... I am waiting... no really, say it **ALOUD** or

I

will

not

continue

with

the

story,..
....
....
....
....
....
....
....
....
....
....YOU*CA...
YOU*CA... LOUDER... YOU*CA... GOOD...OKAY).

Mamita gently swats my hand away and gives me a smile.

"Does everyone have room for dessert?" Tia Lucy suggests.

"Don't be silly, there is always room! What a silly question," Mamita calls out as she clears the table. I also inherited my grandmother's' sweet tooth.

We walk a few blocks down to a tiny little café in the Center of Miraflores. We sit and order *Churros*, a sort of Spanish Doughnut. Refined and highly sophisticated, it is a very distant cousin of the Homer Simpson doughnut, long and slender and covered in sugar. Unlike the unsightly fried dough plop that you get at carnivals in the U.S., the churro can be eaten with dignity and elegance with your pinky finger in the air.

"So how do you feel about going to school?" Tia Rosy questions me.

I mechanically reply, "Okay," when what I really want to say is, "I really don't think I want to start school here and I am nervous and I don't think I will do very well in the classes seeing as my Spanish sucks and I don't even know if Math is the same in Spanish because I have never been to school where everybody speaks Spanish- well the real Spanish, where you go to sleep dreaming in Spanish, not the make pretend Spanish that we speak back home, where my friends are who I miss a lot and I don't know if I will make friends like that here because I really don't even know what people talk about here and what they do for fun after school or if they even like to do the same things that I do because I am from Connecticut and I wasn't raised in Peru."

"Okay," I repeat instead, just in case everyone didn't hear me the first time.

With a knot in my stomach, my appetite for my *churro* quickly fizzles out. Mamita on the other hand is ordering seconds, she's tiny but she can pack it in!

"Can we get a few to go please?" she asks the waiter.

Wanting no more than to stop focusing on my impending doom, I ask for the nearest restroom. Excusing myself, I make my way to the back of the café. One thing that I cannot stand is an unclean restroom. This meant I was shit out of luck since I moved to a third world country. As I turn the doorknob to the bathroom with my sleeve, I am greeted with the stench of urine. In the corner is a miniature woman in a maid's uniform.

"*Buenos dias senorita,*" she says as she bows her head.

"*Buenas.*"

Pointing towards one of the stalls, I gesture to her that she can go ahead of me. Shaking her head she smiles politely and ushers me into the stall with both hands. I crouch over the toilet bowl because the majority of public bathrooms in Peru do not provide the luxury of toilet seats; this is the squat model. Finishing my business, I also realize too late what else is considered a luxury in these facilities. Toilet paper is not a right, it is a privilege. I am still not accustomed to arming myself with a reserve of toilet paper as my aunts are. Getting a cramp in my leg from squatting so long, I can't just get up and leave. Shaking back and forth like a wet dog trying to dry himself, I can only laugh at my situation. Man! The hazards of living in a third world country are endless.

Clearing her throat, I see a tiny hand come under the stall door holding a nicely folded bundle of toilet paper. Relieved that she came to my rescue, I walk out of the stall with a heart full of gratitude. I flash her a grand smile, but as I walk out of the bathroom she slowly puts out her hand.

"Oh, *un minuto*," I reply, flustered, checking my pockets for money I know I don't have. Shrugging my shoulders, I quickly run out the bathroom.

Reaching the table I slide into the booth next to Papi. "Papi, how much is toilet paper worth?"

"Hum, what, what do you mean, how much is a roll?

"No, there is a lady in the bathroom selling squares of toilet paper. How much should I give her for five squares?"

Laughing, Papi pulls out a handful of change. "Give her 10 *centavos* I guess, I don't know."

Grabbing all of Papi's change, I hurry back to the bathroom. I give her all the change, embarrassed that I just paid her to wipe my cuchie.

"*Gracias por el papel Señora.*" The word "*Señora*" slips out because she looks so aged and tired, but as I look at her more closely, I realize she could have easily been my age. What kind of hardship do you have to face that your last resort is selling toilet paper in a restroom? I bet this girl would jump at the chance to attend a private school in Miraflores. I give her a last glance as I walk out.

On our way home Mamita makes it a point to find some hungry soul to feed. She pulls out her doggy bag of *yuquitas* and churros and embraces a young girl on the corner who is begging for money. With appreciation in her eyes, she takes the leftovers with a slight bow of the head and a smile.

Back home I feel drained. My full stomach and new-found appreciation for my privilege of the upcoming experience of school settles inside of me as I get ready to take my daily siesta. Mamita makes her rounds and stops by my bed.

"Something wrong?"

"No, I am okay, really, I'm just nervous about school tomorrow."

"It is okay to be nervous. New experiences break our daily routines. People are nervous of change but it also brings beautiful new things into our lives. A great many people had to overcome their fears to accomplish greatness." She gets up and closes the metal blinds. "Sure, did you know that your *paisano*, Thomas Edison was afraid of the dark? Just think!"

"No, I had no idea, that's funny." She makes the sign of the cross on my forehead.

As my mind races about the upcoming school day, I stare at the bare light bulb on the peeling ceiling, the last thing I see before I eventually fall asleep.

Tummy Button

Herman Melville, author of Moby Dick, called Lima "the saddest city on earth." Looking out of the window of Mamita's car on the way to my first day of school, I agreed. The sun seems reluctant to come up and the early rush hour traffic possesses a dreary lag. The fog lingering in the air slowly seeps into my brain. I kept running first day of school scenarios in my head last night, and didn't get any sleep. Were they going to announce over the loudspeaker that there was a new girl in school? Were people going to pick on me because of my choppy Spanish? Were the nuns going to smack my hands with wooden rulers?

As I walk into the head chancellor's office with Papi and Tia Rosy, I feel like I am going to puke.

"Buenos dias!" a heavy set man with white skin and blondish hair roars as he motions for us to sit.

The conversation is a blur to me as I try to calm the butterflies that are trying to burst out of my stomach. Rubbing my belly to quiet them, I miss what the chancellor is asking me.

"Sorry, what?" I ask to have him repeat his question.

"How-old-are-you?" he asks very slowly, speaking in English with a thick accent.

"Tengo diez y seis años, Senor," I quickly reply, not liking the fact that he thinks I don't know any Spanish. *I am not a lazy, dumb American.*

Explaining that he thinks keeping me back a grade would be in my best interest, he hands Papi a stack of paperwork to fill out. While the chancellor makes small talk with Tia Rosy, I look out the window into the courtyard. It is still early morning and I see lines of students filling the open courtyard in what seems to be an assembly. Looking at the standard uniform, you can tell who the popular girls are. They seemed to have altered their skirts just enough to not get in trouble. With shorter and tighter skirts than the other awkward-looking girls, they make the uniform look fashionable. I look down at my crisp, clean, straight-from-the-uniform-store skirt. I feel like I am wearing one of Mamita's skirts.

"What is your middle name?" Papi says scratching his head with a pencil giving me a smirk.

"Ha ha," I whisper. Papi always disliked his lengthy name, Moises Alberto Yllanes Luza. Trying to save his children from that burden, we all were devoid of the extra weight of a middle name on our birth certificates.

Turning back to the window, I see perfectly uniformed lines of students up and down the courtyard facing the chancellor's office. The chatter ceases and the courtyard becomes dead silent. Waiting for something to happen, I hold my breath. What are they going to do; a show, a reenactment of Grease maybe? Surprisingly, they do break out into song. Far from Grease, I can faintly hear the group sing a song that I find vaguely familiar: our national anthem.

"Somos libres! Seamos lo siempre, seamos lo siempre!" they sing loudly, with emotion. At my old high school, kids wearily recited the pledge of allegiance in a shuffle of quietly mumbled words. A monotony of meaningful words tainted with time. The pride these students radiate is electric; I get chills as I look on sitting up in my seat for a better look, I feel like they are singing to me. The ridiculously long anthem that we call our own (12 verses) does not faze these students as they bring their passion till the end. Later I would realize that the feeling they were all singing to me was because the Peruvian flag was raised on the roof of the chancellor's' office. They were facing my direction, singing praise to *their* red, white, and true.

With a full heart, I turn to Papi and see that he is struggling to fill out the forms without his glasses. He looks stressed and tired. I see right through him and for a moment I see him at my age, in the courtyard singing with all his emotion to a country that he would leave and come back to. Would I ever sing the Peruvian national anthem with that emotion, I wonder? Shit, because right now I don't even know the words.

I reach for the forms so I can help, but Papi shakes his head, pulling the forms out of my reach as he remarks, "No, that's okay Mama, almost finished."

In the main office I meet the secretary, a very tall slender woman with too much makeup who introduces herself as Señora Felix-Diaz and informs me that she is going to show me to my classroom. I say my goodbyes and hold onto Papi a little longer. As I walk out, Tia Rosy blows me a kiss, but Papi keeps walking without glancing back.

"Oh, I forgot my keys, wait here please," Señora Felix-Diaz orders as she disappears behind the counter.

Looking down, I glance at the forms on the counter. Name... age... date of birth... parent's birth names... sibling names... nationality... I get closer to make out Papi's handwriting and... hey, that can't be right.

"Oh there they are I was looking for these!" The chancellor shouts as he snatches the forms from my view. "Have a great first day Ms. New York!"

Maybe I didn't read it right or maybe that wasn't my paperwork, but that did look like Papi's handwriting. Feeling queasy, I follow Señora Felix-Diaz to my classroom. I stay a few steps behind her and quickly roll up the waist of my skirt a few inches so I don't look as awkward as I feel.

Everything is made of stone and the exterior of the school looks like a penitentiary, barbed wire and all. Uninviting and cold, my footsteps echo thunderously down the hallway as we reach the classroom. After an awkward introduction made while standing in front of the class, I take a seat in the first row next to a plump girl with short jet black hair.

"Hello, nice to meet you," she whispers to me in English with a genuine smile.

Keeping my lips tightly shut so that the butterflies in my stomach don't fly out, I smile back.

"Perfect, you are here just in time for our English lesson," the teacher says in Spanish.

"All of your books are inside your desk," the girl next to me whispers.

Lifting the top of my desk, I find the English textbook. Skimming the pages, I try to keep up as the teacher flies through the lesson. She is throwing out adverbs, nouns, prefixes, adjectives, and suffixes as my heart sinks. What the hell is a conjugation? Pretending that I understand perfectly the material being covered, I nod my head every once in a while, making sure not to make eye contact with the teacher. Disappointed with myself for not knowing the English language as well as native Spanish speakers, I am relieved when we are told to put our books away.

Pleased to have a break, I inspect the room. The classroom is as varied as a chocolate assortment box. I spot a tall, pale skinned blonde guy who looks more Austrian than Peruvian. There are quite a few kids who look like they should be named Bret or Stacy. I notice only a handful of the "typical" Indian-looking Peruvians (the ones that grace the cover of National Geographic sporting red cheeks). Scanning a second time, I notice there are absolutely no black kids (no dark chocolate here).

"My name is Marcella," the chubby girl to my left offers, as the classroom gets loud with chatter.

"Ady." I force a smile.

"Where are you from?" she questions, making a clear effort to pronounce each word clearly.

"Connecticut."

"Ay yes, a neighbor with New York, capital is Hartford! Correct?"

Amazed that she would know anything about lil' ole' Connecticut I am surprised. "Yes, you are right. How do you know that?"

"Oh, my aunt lives in New York but we learn capitals of the states in elementary school." Great, not only does she know the English language better than me but she also knows all the capitals of the US states, something that I can say I do not possess. Come on, do *you* know the capital of Missouri? *Who ever heard of Jefferson City!?*

A tap on my shoulder makes me turn around.

"Hi, my names is Luana, nice to see you," a pretty lanky girl with golden, curly, locks declares with a strange Spanish accent.

"Hi, I am Ady."

"Don't worry you can come with us for lunch. Did you..." She pauses as everyone halts to attention, returning to their desks, completely silent and rising to stand tall. Following their lead I stand up as a young man walks into the room. With my eyes forward, I feel like a soldier in the military.

Standing up when the professor walks into the room? No shrieking from the teacher to settle down and please pay attention? *I have fallen into a parallel universe.* Remaining standing until the teacher takes a seat, the students seem genuinely interested in what is coming out of his mouth. As they ask what I perceive as intelligent questions, I notice the classroom as a whole seems to be soaking up the information the teacher is dishing out. Oblivious to what the math lesson is covering, I peer out the window. Cinder blocks and s'more cinder blocks. *Two cinder blocks times two cinder blocks, equal four cinder blocks.*

After an hour of torture by numbers, we are let loose for a bathroom break.

"Come, I will show you the facilities," the chubby girl to my left motions to me with a flick of her hand.

"I will join you as well," Luana says with what sounds like a down-South accent. She sounds like a Southern belle trying to speak Spanish.

"So did you ever meet any famous people? Bon Jovi, Shakira, Michael Jackson? I hear Shakira is super nice, *bien chevere*," Marcella the chubby girl asks, as if they were my neighbors.

"No, I never met anyone famous in my life. Well… except La India on the way over here. She was on the plane sitting in coach with her bodyguards, but I didn't talk to her."

This girl is funny, she starts rambling off questions to me like I stole something.

"Is it true that people bring guns to school?"

"Do you dream in Spanish or English?"

"What exactly is a Crispy Creams?"

"Do you really call your teachers by their first name?"

"Are you baptized?"

"Do you know anyone who has their tummy button pierced?"

"Tummy button?" I ask.

Lifting her shirt revealing her round belly she points, "The button of your tummy?"

Laughing, "Oh yeah, yes I do, my *bellybutton* is pierced."

"*¿Franco?*" she questions.

"What, who's *franco*?" I say confused.

"*Franco*… means for the truth… really?"

"Oh yes, *franco*, I really do." I say as I lift my shirt a little. She covers her mouth in shock at my mutilated bellybutton.

"And this is where we have lunch." She points to an open lounge with flimsy plastic tables and chairs. As we walk by I peer into the large kitchen in the back. The cafeteria ladies (without hairnets) are creating three course meals from scratch. Like a crime scene, I see splatters of real tomatoes on the wall, potato peels passed out on the floor, corn husks strewn about, and flour like gun powder lingering in the air. It is a chaos of nutrition, vitamins, and a well-balanced meal. A small blackboard displays the *menú* for the day: *Rellena de Papa o Cau Cau, Ensalada Rusa, y Arroz con Leche*. No day old rubbery, microwave sausage and egg breakfast sandwiches? I am going to partake in omelets made with eggs straight from the chicken. I can practically see the cheerful chicken squatting above the frying pan.

"Oh yuck, Peruvian food is so bland," Luana remarks.

"Luana is from Brazil, she hates Peruvian food."

"I will prefer a bowl of *Feijoada* over *Cau Cau* any day," she declares.

Making it out alive at the end of the school day, I feel more at ease, and manage to shrug away the feelings of uncertainty. Maybe this sad, poor, overcast country is actually livable. Sneaking up to the roof of Mamita's house, I pull my sweater tight around me as I gaze out over the edge. I am comforted by the commotion of the everyday hullabaloo down below that I found so strange when I first arrived. Feeling like I am being watched, I look around and spot the moon. One thing that stayed constant in my whirlwind of transcontinental hopping is the sun and the moon. Mother Moon... *Mama Quilla* is essential for calculating the passage of time. *Protector of women... cried tears of silver*. How much time will have to pass for me to find out?

Pregnant Lexicon

"There's daggers in men's smiles."

"Those that listen, get addicted to my diction."

"We know what we are, but know not what we may be."

"Pure knowledge expands from my esophagus, I write here tonight to bring truth to the light."

Can you distinguish the eloquent prose of Shakespeare from the contemplative flow of a talented rapper? Do the words of a sixteenth century dead man carry more weight than a rags-to-riches rapper in the twentieth century? When the words hit the paper like lightning, do they bounce back at you and ignite a spark in your brain? I liken reading to getting pregnant: the words fertilize your mind and give birth to ideas that were not a part of you before their conception. Sadly, just like women who are born infertile, there are people that never are able to fertilize their minds. I hope as you read my story you get 'pregnant' at least a few times.

Centuries before the meaningful lyrics of Rock-a-fella- Jay-Z, the creator of Roca Wear- came the even more profound Inca Roca. Inca Roca was the 6th Sapa Inca of Cuzco in the year 1350. He was said to have established the *Yachaywasi*, a school for teaching nobles. *Yachaywasi* in Quechua means "house of learning". Some people can interpret the word "learning" at face value and picture a student sitting at a desk as a teacher lectures. Not aware of it at the time, or until years later, my *Yachaywasi* was soon to come as my family decided to go on a roadtrek East of Lima to where my parents originally began their existence.

I have never been to Mount Rushmore, The Grand Canyon, or Yellowstone National Park. Though I lived in the U.S. all my life, I never had an interest to visit those national monuments. I do not think looking at a huge crack in the ground or sitting in a tent waiting for Yogi Bear to steal my picnic basket is entertainment.

Lounging on the hard couch in Mamita's living room staring out the steel barred window, I ask, "Papi I was reading about *Las Lineas de Nazca*. Is that very far from here? That sounds like a cool place."

"About five hours south. I've never been," he replies, while munching on *habas* (toasted and peeled fava beans).

The Nazca Lines are a series of huge drawings of geometrical figures and animals ranging up to 1,000 feet large that are etched into the dry desert floor in Nazca, Peru. They were not noticed until 1939, when a North American scientist flew over them in a small plane. There is a huge spider, a monkey, geometric shapes, and a series of parallel lines that people believe to be a landing strip for aliens. How they were made, when, and by who is a scientific mystery.

"Do you think that aliens made them?" I question, looking back at Papi.

"I don't think that extraterrestrials need a landing strip to mark their way to a safe landing. I would hope their technology is far too advanced for that."

"So what do you think they are, like who made them?"

"Oh, I don't know for sure. One theory is that they are a solar calendar made from the constellations, which makes the most sense to me."

"We had calendars thousands of years ago; why are Peruvians always late then?"

He points to his simple Casio watch and shrugs his shoulders. "You want to go to the *lineas*? We can try to make a trip a few more places if we are going to drive that far."

We decide that a road trip would be a good idea, since there is a weeklong break from school coming up. Recruiting a handful of relatives that want to join, we gather a small army and start making plans.

We had been living in Lima for a few months and still had not visited Bianca and Guille, but we finally get the okay from Pachi to visit. We enter the gated community of Chaclacayo, 45 minutes from Mamita's house, checking in with the armed guard. I wonder how Bianca will react to my father and me. It had been almost ten months since we had seen each other.

Bianca is the one who answers the door. She stands there with a glimmer in her eye, and when she sees Papi she runs into his arms and exclaims, "*Tio* Moises!"

I stand back as they say their hellos, hurt that she just called him uncle.

"*Hola Ady! ¿Como estas?*" she shrieks as she gives me a huge lingering hug. She is a little more slender and a tad taller now. She looks years older to me.

As we make our way into the house we are greeted by Pachi, Lorena, and Guille. In between small talk about the trip and the weather, there are breaks of awkward silence. Sitting there watching Bianca steal curious glances at Papi, I feel sad that we are in this situation. Like a big pink elephant in the room the conversation never turns to the fact that Bianca had mysteriously developed amnesia. Had she really forgotten?

After a delicious lunch of potato leek soup I go outside with Bianca and Guille. They grab their bikes and I watch as they ride up and down the dusty road.

"Watch this Ady!" Bianca shouts in Spanish as she races up the tiny hill with her tricycle with all her might.

"That was cool, good job!" I cheer in English.

She smiles politely but doesn't respond.

"She only speaks Spanish, she doesn't speak English with anybody here," Guille clarifies, wiping the sweat from his forehead. "They don't talk about it, they didn't tell her," he adds, shaking his head as he walks away.

I want to pull Bianca aside and ask if she remembers us, if she remembers the house on Ginger Lane, but I don't have the heart to. We stay for a few hours and gently leave, as if not to disrupt the mirage that they created for my sister, nestled between the looming mountains above their house. Papi drives home in silence. He lost his daughter amidst a mountain of lies.

Lorena explains later that the reason for her deception was for the good of Bianca. She did not want her to feel alienated in her own house. How would she have explained to a five year old the dynamics of her situation? The branches of our family tree were beginning to intertwine into an undecipherable mess. Confusing enough for an adult to comprehend, it would have been too much for a five year old to grasp. So, Papi was magically transformed into *Tio* Moises... until her sixteenth birthday when she found out the truth on a little road trip.

Lima la Horrible

Like a 3-D alarm clock, the earth shakes my bed gently to wake me on the day we are leaving on our mini-excursion south. By now the mini-earthwobbles are a part of my daily routine, and I learn to keep my balance. Living on the geological fault line *Cadena Del Fuego*, a mini quake is my cup of coffee in the morning. You want a big thrill like bungee jumping, base jumping, or playing with poisonous snakes? Try living in a third world country for a while, there are thrills lurking around every corner.

Up at the crack of dawn, me, Papi, six of my favorite aunts and uncles, and my grandmother pack up our things. We rented a minibus for the occasion that looks like Scooby Doo's Mystery Machine. The chilly mist threatens our vision as we start packing the van.

"Which wine goes best with roadside food Pepe, white or red?" Tia Rosy questions my Uncle Pepe, holding up two bottles.

"One for you, one for me," he replies slowly as if he were really contemplating. He then grabs them both and places them gingerly next to his bottle of Pisco. I hope they don't try to take a drunken joyride in this monster of a machine.

I grab a ham (real ham, *jamon serrano*, the best aged pig around) and cheese (straight milk-from-the-cow cheese, not processed American cheese) sandwich and run upstairs to get my toothbrush. Making my way back via the concrete spiral staircase on the patio, I hear my name spoken in a whisper.

"… why… wait so many years to tell Ady… the past is gone…" *Mamita* speaks softly.

"… perfect opportunity… should know about her family," Papi replies.

Had I been bold enough, I would have ran down the stairs and demanded to know what Papi had to share with me. Had I been a more audacious character, I would have interrupted their conversation. Instead, like the cowardly lion, I tiptoe back up the staircase and go back down the main stairs to the front of the house instead. Like a marble in my brain, the possibilities of what they were referring to keep rolling around in my head.

"Here, take these, you can use them as pillows until we need them," Tia Lucy says, handing me a few packages of toilet paper. *We are resourceful.*

Squeezing into the back of the van, I make sure I sit next to the window. I am a lowly traveler who suffers from motion sickness.

"Everyone ready to go? Do we have everything?" Papi calls over his shoulder from the driver's seat.

"Oh, one moment!" Mamita shouts a little too loudly from her seat in the middle. She bows her head, *"Creo en Dios, Padre todopoderoso, creador del Cielo y de la Tierra…. En el nombre del Padre, y del Hijo, y del Espíritu Santo. Amén.* Okay we can proceed."

My grandmother is so religious she often needs God's approval to sneeze. Protected by the safety bubble of Mamita's prayer to the Father Almighty, we head east towards the Center of Lima. The city is already awake at this early hour, with people clogging the streets. The wave of pollution blocks our nasal passages as we drive deeper into Lima; "Lima la horrible", as the famous Peruvian writer Mario Vargas Llosa describes it during the winter months.

There is a ridiculously loud banging at the back of the van as we stop at a red light. A couple of young men holding bootleg videos are trying to climb on top of the van. Alarmed that they are going to rob us, my dad shouts out his window and makes a quick movement to jump out of the van. My heart is in my throat as we speed away, running the red light before a fight can break out. Later we would realize that the two men were in cahoots with another young gentleman who quickly grabbed my aunt's garage door opener from the passenger side visor as we all looked back at the commotion. *Brilliant thieves!*

Getting robbed marked us like a going away present as we leave the chaos of Lima. The air gets clearer as we drive south, and the sun peeks out a bit. Getting comfortable, I stretch out and rest my head on the toilet paper rolls while my feet rest on my grandmother's lap. I look to the front and catch Papi looking at me from the rearview mirror. I hope the secret he is keeping from me is as simple as, "Your middle name is really Eulalia." I close my eyes and try not to think about the varied possibilities. Maybe... but how can I not be a part of this family? I have to be... I am... Yllanes.

Bugs Bunny

What a beautiful dream. I sit and feel the heat of the sun on my face. *The colors are so brilliant.* I marvel as the panorama races by my vision. The neon green, blinding orange, and fiery red plant life look like they flew right off a painting. *I must be stuck inside a painting.* I hear a loud rustling of leaves behind me and turn quickly to see what has been following me. I must have turned too quickly as I bump my head. *Shit!* The thump of my head on the window of the minibus painfully jolts me out of my slumber. I must have been at least half awake though, because the view outside is just as beautiful as my dream. Sitting up in my seat, the toilet paper roll that is semi-stuck to my cheek makes the same rustling noise that snuck into my dream.

There have been studies that indicate that highly intelligent people are able to dream in color. Those of the lesser knowledge persuasion tend to dream in only black and white. So try to remember tonight if you dream in color or not. Also, don't believe everything you read; this is completely fabricated and amusing to think that you would try to formulate color into your dream scheme.

I rise as we pass a beautiful paradise. This scenery is breathtaking; a far leap from the dirt and garbage littered streets of Lima. The blue sky is clear and the sun is able to shine through the fluffy white clouds without a problem. The beams of sunlight are hitting the perfectly manicured plots of green grass. The soft natural brown of the mountain is beautifully contrasted with the vibrant green of the vegetation. The animals are out to graze and as they look up at me they seem to be smiling!

"Papi where are we?"

"About only three hours south of Lima, still a long way to go. We are going to stop soon to grab a bite to eat."

"Water?" Tio Pepe offers handing me a bottle of Pisco. Pisco is our national alcoholic beverage, the finest in the world... depending on who you ask. Ask a Chilean where the best Pisco is made.

I shake my head for fear of alcohol poisoning.

"Don't worry, really, it is purified water, we finished the Pisco hours ago!" he says slurring his words, holding up a packet of water purification tablets.

Taking a swig of the chemical flavored water, I sit up and lean my head on my grandmother's shoulder.

"Did you sleep well?" My grandmother looks to the side handing me a piece of chocolate. *Where does she store all this candy?* She must have little elves that work for her.

"Yes, great."

"Good, you are going to need your strength," she says, squeezing my hand giving me a look of what I take to be sympathy.

"I am starving!" Tia Rosy sings melodically in a shrill, inebriated tone. "Let's get some *picarones*! I smell *picarones*!"

Papi pulls over to a little shack on the side of the gorgeous mountain we are scaling. As we pile out of the van I realize that we must look like a mass of clowns climbing out of the tiny van; there are so many of us. I take a long, profound breath of the clean mountain air. Stretching my legs and lifting my arms up to crack my back, I catch sight of a beautiful little girl playing in the dirt on the side of the road. She looks to be a little older than Bianca, and she is playing with a dirty cloth doll. She is so close to the main road the speeding traffic makes her long black hair blow into her face. Petrified that she is so close to the road, I make eye contact with her and motion for her to come to where I am standing. After a while she walks towards me, eyes downcast. Glad she is out of harm's way, I ask her, "What is your name?"

She smiles at me with her red cheeks and dark eyes. She nods her head and keeps on smiling; she is beautiful. Before she can reply, her mother calls for her and she skips to the shack.

There is no floor in the restaurant/shack, only dirt, and the walls are recycled slabs of wood and aluminum. They have a makeshift grill made out of stones and wood, and whatever is cooking smells mouth-watering.

"Do you want *anticucho*?" Papi asks as he comes up behind me, startling me. "Maybe you should just eat something light, I don't know if our stomachs are used to the food yet. You really do not want to get an upset stomach while we are traveling."

I longingly look at the *anticuchos* on the grill. *Anticuchos* are skewers made from beef heart, marinated in Peruvian spices and grilled. It looks like a shish kabob or a Puerto Rican pincho. I guess no *anticuchos* for me; I don't want to be glued to the crapper the whole trip.

Grabbing a variety of fresh fruits and a roll of bread instead, I join my aunts outside. They are sitting under a tent next to a tiny old woman who is preparing *picarones* from scratch. *Picarones* are fried doughnut-shaped pastries made from mashed sweet potato. She is cooking with an old rusty looking vat of boiling oil, but she is cooking so quickly that I almost don't register her unsanitary cooking method. Unfortunately, the sweet smell of pastries do not make up for the fact that she is washing the dirty dishes, quickly throwing the batter into the oil with her bare hands, and then returning to the dishes. Food sanitation guidelines do not reach this far up into the mountains, I guess. I fabricate a food safety inspector with glasses standing next to this old woman shaking his head while tearing up his clipboard with red marker.

"Here, try some, it is delicious," Tia Lucy exclaims.

"No, that's okay, Papi said maybe I shouldn't eat anything heavy."

"You sure? It's covered in *Chancaca*." *Chancaca* is a very sweet sugarcane syrup.

Not wanting to eat anything with the word caca in it, on top of the soapy batter, I politely decline.

"Tia, the bathroom?" I ask instead.

She points to a small tiled wall in the distance.

I run to the minivan and grab a roll of toilet paper, thrilled at the fact that I am well equipped for my peepee excursion. I am getting the hang of things after all.

As soon as I enter the bathroom, I am immediately confused. The circular tile and wooden stall is enclosed, there's no roof, and the dirt floor is bare minus a gaping hole the size of a football. Unbelievable, someone stole the freaking toilet bowl! Inspecting the scene of the crime, I can still smell the nasty remnants of the missing latrine. *Maybe I should just piss in the hole!* As I encounter more of these kinds of restrooms on the side of the road I will eventually realize that the toilet was never thieved; that was exactly the purpose of the hole. It was a squat-n-piss-hole.

Disappointed, I walk towards the minivan and climb on the hood. The rolling mountains and blue sky look like they are made of a paint that can never be replicated by a human. The enormous scale of the view is indescribable. My eyeballs hurt from trying to take it all in. I take another deep breath of smog-free air and jump off the hood.

I almost crush the little girl from earlier who is now standing at my feet.

"Ah, sorry, are you okay!?"

She regains her balance and doesn't reply, she just smiles and keeps her head down as she kicks at the dirt with her little sandals.

"What is your name?" I ask again for the second time.

She shakes her head, shrugs her shoulders, and then nods her head. Maybe she is deaf, or maybe she doesn't speak Spanish. We are in the mountains, so maybe she speaks Quechua.

Tio Pepe stumbles by singing a little ditty, and I ask, "Tio, can you ask her what her name is in Quechua?"

"What is your name?" After no response he questions, also in Quechua, "Is that a llama eating your shoe?" But still, she says nothing. "This little thing does not have a clue what I am talking about. Hey, what is wrong with the little peanut? She don't talk much?" he shouts to her mother, who is passing by with an armful of dirty dishes.

The mother exchanges words with Tio Pepe in Quechua. Sounding like Jabba the Hutt (the fictional Huttese language in Star Wars is largely based on the Quechua language), she nods her head and frowns as she looks down at the little girl.

"Ah, poor child, that must be hard," Tio Pepe replies in Spanish, climbing into the van and tapping the top of the girl's head.

I notice as I move back and forth that she is following the movement of my body. Soon I realize that she is entranced with the Bugs Bunny I have embroidered on my button down shirt.

I point to it, "Bugs Bunny?" I stick out my front teeth like a bunny. "Bunny? *Conejo*. Bugs Bunny? Do you have bunny's way up here in the mountains?" I hop around in a circle putting my hand on my backside, wagging my imaginary bunny tail.

She laughs an innocent playful laugh, and then quickly covers her mouth as if she surprised herself with the noise that she created.

"Do you like it?" I mimic in my best Bugs Bunny impersonation while pretending to hold a carrot, "What's up doc?"

From the surroundings it seems to me that she has never seen a functioning television, let alone a cartoon. I think she is very amused with my antics.

As my clan gathers, I turn to the little girl. The last one to get into the van, I kneel down and whisper to her, "Uh… okay… I am leaving now… I am going with my family on a road trip to where my mother and father grew up… it is far, far away. It was nice meeting you. Uh… I know you don't understand me but… or maybe you do understand but… don't tell anyone… well I don't think that you ever will, you don't seem to say much… but my father is going to tell me something on this road trip and I am scared about what it is. I don't think it is good news because he has kept it a secret for such a long time… and I keep thinking about what I saw on the paperwork for school… deep down inside I think maybe he is going to tell me something… that maybe he isn't my real father. You saw him, I don't look anything like him, right? …or anyone in my family. Well… um."

She is hanging on my every word as she leans in towards me, staring at me as if she thinks I am going to vanish into thin air any second.

"What do I do with that information? Really, I don't know what I will do. I guess my family is family, no matter how I got here in the first place, right? They will always be there for me no matter where I originally came from, true?" I nod my head to see if she agrees.

She makes no movement as I stand up to go. I unbutton my shirt and wrap it around her, leaving me only in a tiny tank top. My shirt is long and reaches her ankles, but I can tell she is ecstatic. She twirls around as if she is wearing a beautiful gown, and then she motions for me to come closer.

She quickly looks around and whispers, "Adeline."

How in the world does she know my name? I never told her, I am sure of it.

"Wha..?" I say, baffled.

She reads the confusion in my face, and leans in closer, "My- name- is- Adeline." She skips off again towards the shack not looking back.

As we pull away, the shack becomes a little dot in the distance. I look out the window at the incredibly immense outdoors. The landscape is like no other I have ever seen before. The clouds are gigantic elephants, whales, and llamas, jumping from here to there. There seems to be more room in the sky here for them to prance about.

I look over to my grandmother who is quietly counting prayers on her rosary with her eyes closed. I scoot over to her and rest my head on her shoulder. *How can this person not be my flesh and blood?* We are one in the same. Her likes are my likes, her dislikes mine as well. This can't be learned behavior because my grandmother and I have always lived thousands of miles apart. What else can it be but genetics? It's not scientifically proven but she passed down to me the I-don't-like-fish-gene and the if-I-sit-in-one-place-too-long-I-instantly-fall-asleep-gene.

As I slowly doze off I hear Tio Pepe in the backseat, "... just appeared at the top of the mountain one day. Nobody knows where she came from or who left her there. She was around three years old, left on the side of the road, barefoot with only thin, pajamas with rabbit footsies. The woman who took her in says that the doctor can't find any reason why she shouldn't be speaking. She says something must be wrong with her voice box or her brain because she has never heard her make any sound. Poor girl must have been severely traumatized... never uttered a word in her entire life."

Baby Mummies

Peru possesses the highest navigable lake in the world. The oldest University in the New World is in Lima: *Universidad National de San Marcos.* The earliest known urban center of the Americas is in Caral, 200 kilometers north of Lima. Peru is also the only South American country that possesses mountain highland, jungle, *and* desert. Yet with all the rich history and natural wonders, what is the first thing that comes to mind when you think of when you hear the word Peru? Quick, say it out loud!

Llamas. Freakin' **LLAMAS**, llamas *y mas* llamas. Well world, truth be told, llamas originated from the central plains of North America about 40 million years ago! Some theories reveal camelids originated in *North America* and then traveled north across the Bering land bridge before evolving into camels. Camelids that migrated to the south became the "llama" family. A fossilized llama believed to be 9 million years old was found in Florida. So next time you see a llama, ask them if they hail from South Beach.

I have nothing against llamas, llamas are super cool animals. They truly are a part of our rich history; without them a lot would not have been accomplished. These buck tooth beasts are not all we are, however, I think as I stare into the huge black eyes of one. I was sitting alone in the van after we pulled over for another rest stop and I'd just cracked open the window when a llama craned his humongous neck into the van.

"Papi help!!" I scream at the top of my lungs.

Laughing uncontrollably, he runs to my rescue, shooing the creature away. The llama strolls nonchalantly away, looking back at me as if saying: *What are you doing here? You not from these parts.*

We finally reach our first destination, the small coastal town of Paracas, and climb out of the van feeling like sardines. The tribe stretches out and we leave our belongings in a cramped, musty hotel room. Making sure to take all our valuables (my aunts sport hideous fanny packs), we make our way to the nearest lookout point. We are atop a steep cliff that juts down into a deadly drop to the crystal blue water below. With nothing more than a tiny stone barrier between us and the fall, I lean in for a better view of the ocean.

"Careful, Adelita, we do not need anything to happen to you too," Mamita says as she gently grabs my arm.

"Huh, what do you mean *too*?" I question as I move away from my impending death.

"I said we don't need anything to happen *to you*," she clarifies as she walks away.

You too, I heard her say, you too. My mind roams as I follow the herd of Yllanes' down the sandy path. I walk behind Mamita, stepping into the impression of her footprints in the sand. We are even the same shoe size.

Deciding that we are all on the brink of starvation, we stop at an outdoor restaurant on the beach. The clear blue sky and fresh ocean breeze is a perfect backdrop for our family dinner. The menu is an array of seafood, more seafood than the Pacific. Like a straight person in a sensational gay bar; it is too bad that I despise seafood. Mamita and I decide on splitting a simple spaghetti dish with butter and parmesan cheese. By the end of dinner I sample a bit of shark that is surprisingly soft, and sea turtle that tastes like steak. Feeling terribly guilty about the turtle, I quietly send a prayer to him in turtle heaven. *Amen.*

"Let's visit the museum down the road while we wait. We can't go on the boat tour until an hour after we eat," Tia Rosy remarks.

"That's swimming, Flaca. You are not supposed to *swim* until an hour after you eat," Papi corrects her.

"Well then you go and get sick, I am going to the museum of the mummies," she huffs as she twirls around, smacking him with her huge fanny pack.

We walk along a sandy path under the scorching sun until we reach a sign that is marked "Mumy Museom" on a wooden plank with faded black marker. The tour guide, a young boy about my age wearing a New Kids on the Block t-shirt, speaks in Spanish and English for the other tourists who are in the group. We are walking on the burial grounds of the ancient Paracas culture that thrived in 700 BC. Although interesting and informative, all I can think about is the movie *Poltergeist* as I keep my eyes on the ground and look for unearthed stray skeleton hands. I try to hear what the guide is covering but I can't catch what he is saying in either his too-fast Spanish or his broken English.

Trying to make my way to the front so I can hear him better, I trip and almost push him down a winding staircase in the ground. Catching his balance he gives me an evil glare and continues with the tour.

"Dis is a catacomb that just recently discover. As ju can clearly see here da dirt winding staircase where entirely decorated wif stones and ceramic pice for adornation. An attention to detail is apparent. Please follow me to da burial ground below de surface."

As we follow him down, the winding staircase gets narrower and narrower. We reach the bottom where there is a tiny room hollowed out in the earth. Atop wooden tables are several cloth bundles being held up in sitting position by wooden sticks. I study a few of them. I was expecting the kind of mummies you see in the movies, always in golden coffins looking regal in their deathness. These mummies look like poor beggars that were caught in a snowstorm. On one table is what looks to be a Mommy Mummy, a Papa Mummy, and right in between them is a tiny bundle, a baby mummy. What could this poor fragile baby have died of, I wonder? Was he ill or was there an accident that caused his premature death? Who was spared that had to bury the parents and the baby all together? Whatever it was, the death of an infant must have been devastating for the family even if it was such a very long time ago.

We go on the boat ride just as the day is wrapping up and coming to a colorful end. Content, I look toward the back of the boat that embraces just a small part of my family unit. Laughing and cracking jokes, my aunts' and uncles' faces are illuminated by the orange and red of the setting sun. The brilliant colors highlight the facial features that I am lacking. Their highbrow and cheekbones are nothing like mine. I look over to Mamita, who is smiling at the same view that I am taking in. She is beautiful but I look nothing like her either, one would never take us for relatives.

Their laughing is contagious and I start to laugh along with my aunts and uncles. My giggles come from deep inside, from a part of me that doesn't want to recognize what is right in front of me. We reach the soft sandy shore and as we disembark the stars decide to come out. I recall an image of the Little Prince on his small, lonely planet with his one red rose.

"'When you look up at the sky at night, since I'll be living on one of them, since I'll be laughing on one of them, for you, it'll be as if all the stars are laughing. You'll have stars that can laugh!

And he laughed again.'"

Mickey Mouse Wings

So this would be the part of the storyline when the protagonist of this novel revels in a quick and painless awakening. She... me... Adeline... suddenly realizes the meaning of life and her purpose on this earth. Yes, with this family excursion I attain enlightenment and go on living my teenage years in uninterrupted harmony. But this is no ordinary book; like the book in the NeverEnding Story, this book is quite different. Not furry-dragons-come-flying-out-at-you different, but different because this is not your average story. _This is my life._

The next few days are jam packed with various activities and more driving than The Indy 500, and I feel like I am in and out of consciousness. Peru is massive, it is about the size of Alaska and twice as big as Texas. Like I said before, if I sit in one place too long I automatically fall asleep. I don't have narcolepsy, really, I just love sleep.

In between my episodes of coma, we stop in the Laguna de Huacachina. Huacachina is a tiny Peruvian village built around a natural oasis on the outer fringes of a barren desert. The population is an estimated 200 inhabitants, 50 of them being lizards. Legend holds that the lagoon was created when a beautiful native princess was apprehended by a young hunter, while taking a bath. She quickly fled; leaving the pool of water she had been bathing in to become the lagoon. The folds of her towel, streaming behind her as she ran, became the surrounding sand dunes. The woman is rumored to still live in the oasis as a mermaid, a Peruvian Ariel.

We walk around the lagoon and hit the sand dunes to go sand surfing. Sitting at the top of a huge sand dune with a snow board, not knowing what to do, I close my eyes and throw myself down. The descent is exhilarating! I am barely able to keep myself on the board, constantly losing my balance as I go crashing head first into the soft sand.

"Hey, keep on your toes, you don't want to end up in the lagoon!" my uncle calls out laughing. They all joke about the mermaid that still lives in the lagoon, the one who would drown one person a year as a sacrifice to the lake gods who protect her. *Not funny, not your average fairy tale.*

While on the road, sleep deprivation, heavy drinking, and boredom make for interesting conversation in the van.

"You know, I have not seen one fat person since we have been living in Peru. I mean, there are big people, portly well-fed people here, but not like grossly obese like in the U.S. Not skin falling and flesh hanging down fat, I mean."

"Americans are lazy. They eat fast food and drive there to get it," came shooting out from the back of the van.

"They don't burn calories and they eat garbage. We eat healthy homemade food and walk everywhere!" Was another observation from an unseen face in the back.

"Remember that new Burger King on Javier Prado that opened up last year? People were curious so they went. There were lines of people walking up to the drive thru window!"

"Ah, ridiculous, why pay 30 soles for a burger and fries if you can get a whole three course meal at the corner restaurant for 13 soles. Fancy garbage, that's what it is."

"America's favorite vegetable is the French fry!"

Observations being thrown from all corners of the van, Mamita leans over and whispers to me, "There is nothing wrong with the fat peoples. They are human too, are they not? Just because you are American doesn't mean that you will grow to be a fat lady too." She discreetly hands me a toffee.

"Pass the glass!"

"Where is the wine?"

"I have to pee."

A few long hours later we reach our long-awaited destination. There are no oversized signs or fancy neon lights marking The Nazca Lines. We pull up to a small metal hangar where we seem to be the only ones around for miles. I feel like I am in an old western movie. *Howdy, pilgrim.* I see mirages of tumbleweeds and men with stink eyes as we look around for signs of life.

Dry, dead land as far as the eye can see. I stand up straight and bend down to touch my toes, twirling my arms from side to side in an attempt to crack my back. *RELIEF!* I also have to take a serious pee. I scan the area for a hole in the ground.

"HELLO! HELLO! Anyone home?" my uncle shouts at the top of his lungs. The barren desert swallows his shouts and sucks them into a magical vacuum.... WHOOSH! ++++++++++++++++++++++++
++
++
++
++
++
++
++

Sorry, I got sucked up into the vacuum vortex for a minute. Uh...more like six months. My fingers haven't hit the keys for six long hard months. But just like riding a bike, my fingers slow but steady are hitting the magical keys once again. Creating words and emotions by stringing together the A-B-C's I learned as a preschooler. A pure miracle this writing thing can be if put into the trusting hands of a person who is equipped to tell their story. Akin to a weapon, it has to be used properly, otherwise you end up with broken, jagged words on Facebook that tell a story of not only how you are "macking rice and chicen for diner tonite for my boo" but also tell a tale of the kind of economically-disadvantaged education that plagues our society. Your syntax errors become grenades.

I got lost for a while and strayed off the path of life but I was able to locate a map that my daughter Aymara delivered to me and I found my way back to the road. Sounds crazy but my left hand got chopped off unexpectedly... One Love. Got the floor pulled out from under me and I landed in a position quite unfamiliar to me. "Made my life come to a halt, you stuck me in a dark cave that day because of your genetic predisposition." But that chapter of my life is actually another story that will be told once I am clear out of this fog of failure. I will tell it from the other side so that I can bring light to others who are confused and lost, who can't match words to the ugly side of the real world we live in. I was off the hook for a while but ready to pick up the phone again with my right hand and take a long deep breath...

"HELLO! HELLO! Anyone home?" my uncle shouts at the top of his lungs. The barren desert swallows his shouts and sucks them into a magical vacuum.... WHOOSH!

After a long while of reverse-echo yelling, a tired looking man wearing sunglasses and a dark blue mechanic suit adorned with black grease smudges appears from behind the hangar.

"Yes hello there, how can I help you?" he directs to Tio Pepe.

"Good day, just wondering where the nearest Wong is located?" Pepe jokes with a grin, scanning the obviously barren immense desert, shielding his eyes from the sun with his right hand.

With a dry smirk and an obvious lack of humor, he turns to Papi instead and asks, "Are you looking for a tour guide?"

"Why yes we are. Can you direct us to someone that can show us the lines?"

Slowly peeling off his mechanic outfit, he reveals an army-green button down shirt with matching pants. A tiny pin with droopy looking wings is dangling from his shirt. *The pilot and the mechanic.* Bloody hell, maybe the plumber too? "My name is Inigo Montoya, I will be your pilot for the day, prepare to fly." He points to the pin with wings as if it were a pilot's license.

After much debate, we decide to go with the Mickey Mouse pilot and his plastic wings of proof.

The take-off is terrifyingly turbulent. The one propeller plane can only hold four people, so I go with Papi and Tia Maruja. For a while I don't dare look out the window for fear of my motion sickness coming to a climax and making me have to puke in the tightly confined area.

When I am finally able to keep my visual balance, I look out and see a whole bunch of nothin'. I know we didn't just drive this whole way to see a bunch of green and brown land. *I can see this in Connecticut.* After a half hour of nothingness I question the pilot, who is making small circles around the same pieces of land.

Shouting in his right ear I inquire, "Excuse me, when are we going to get to the *Lineas*?"

"Oh, sorry, I thought that you were enjoying them. Usually this is a spiritual journey for people who do not want to be interrupted with mindless banter. Gringos usually meditate and want to become one with the land. I thought that was what you were doing."

Was I that obviously a gringa?

He goes on to explain as he begins to point out the almost hidden figures, "You see there on that side of that mountain? That is what they call the astronaut. You can see the human form with a helmet like shape on his head. I personally think it looks like an extraterrestrial."

As soon as he points it out, I see it. They pop up from the ground like magic once he waves his finger over them. The ground that looked so common a second ago comes alive with animals: a hummingbird, a spider, a monkey, and a condor. Like an animated cartoon, they begin to move as we circle around them. The sheer immensity of the figures boggles my mind. What tools did they need and how many people had to gather to create these figures on enormous mountains? Were they drinking hallucinogenic cactus juice or humbly paying homage to their gods?

"Papi, it looks like an enormous Etch-A-Sketch, don't you think?"

Shit, if our people were so advanced more than 2,000 years ago why is Lima still stuck in the dark ages? With motivation and skill like this we should be number one in the world by now. I can't spot that drive and determination in the people that drag along in the streets of Lima. Maybe it got lost, misplaced for a while like a treasure waiting to be unearthed again... maybe it is buried here in the sand somewhere. Someone just has to hunt for it, find it, and dig it up.

As we descend *I do* start to feel a spiritual connection with the earth. I have a tickle in my belly that made me feel like there is more out there. The impossible is truly possible. *The things we-make-make -us*. What can I possibly create, discover, or uncover in my lifetime that can measure up to this legacy that was left for us in the desert? I cannot fathom what I will one day unearth for myself.

"It's here that the little prince appeared on Earth, then disappeared. What makes the desert beautiful," says the little prince, *"is that somewhere it hides a well."*

Time in the Foundation

The ride leaving Nazca is hauntingly beautiful. As we make our way northeast the scenery changes dramatically. The browns and oranges switch channels to greens and yellows. The Lion King African Plains turn into Alice in Wonderland Brilliant Technicolor. I imagine Rafiki the monkey from The Lion King questioning, *"Who are you?"* The Caterpillar from Alice in Wonderland peeks out through the yellow bushes on the side of the road, *"Who are you?"* A few hours of driving in a car with no radio will do that to you. Barren desert mirages play in your head and turn your brain waves into electric shocks.

Mindless banter due to boredom resumes; and action!

"Can we plug in the blender somewhere? Let's make some Pisco Sour!"

"Hey did you see that? It looked like a kangaroo. We don't have kangaroos... do we?"

"How come I haven't seen any mentally challenged Peruvians? Do we not have that gene? "

"Oh we have them; they are just shut in the house. To have them out in public would bring shame on the family. We don't have any in our family."

"If they are born in the Amazonia they still practice 'canoe capsizing'. When a handicapped or mentally challenged child is born, they are eliminated by capsizing the canoe. The canoe is turned over and the child falls into the river."

"Brutal!"

"Por Dios!"

I am relieved for a minute that I didn't inherit any fat, retarded genes. But if this isn't my biological family is there a possibility that I *could* grow up to be a delayed rolly polly? My thoughts wander to the darkest parts of my mind.

"Oh my bejesus!" Aunt Lucy exclaims while grasping her chest.

"Is it your heart?" my grandmother asks in a concerned voice, while holding onto her own chest.

Looking around, I see everyone's faces change to sheer panic. Cracking the windows and taking off layers of jackets, I feel as if I missed a very important memo.

"Ady calm down and relax, sit back and concentrate on your breathing," Tia Rosy instructs as she puts the back of her hand to her forehead.

Looking to Papi's face in the driver's rear view mirror I throw him a questioning look, as he peers back at me with a grin. He mumbles in quick, choppy English so that no one would catch his, "Just do it." He continues in Spanish, "Mama, we are driving up one of the very highest access highways in Peru. The high altitude can cause shortness of breath and slowness of the heart beating." He is concentrating on the road but I can see his amused smile in the rearview mirror.

Truth is, I don't feel any change in my heartbeat or the quality of the air. I really hope that I am not going to suffocate up here in the barren mountains. A heart attack and asphyxiation at age 16 doesn't sound natural. I prefer to die a little old biddy in a rocking chair, not at the top of a killer mountain. *Danger lurking around every corner when you are living in a third world country.*

As we climb the murderous mountain the van is solemnly silent. Everyone is concentrating on their breathing and their dangerously pulsating hearts. We soon reach the summit, where we are greeted by the sign, "Vista de Omni Aqui".

We climbed the impossible mountain in the Mystery Machine to reach the climatic: "Alien Lookout Point". Unidentified flying objects have been seen on this peak more than Elvis in Vegas. UFO fanatics from all over the world flock to this particular overpass just to stand by the road and possibly catch a glimpse of E.T. We just happened to pass by it on our way to the town where my mom and father had met so many years ago. I look up to the sky for a second, wishing we could be lucky enough to catch a big-headed, green, one-eyed creature streaking by in a shiny metal saucer, maybe wearing one of those Peruvian hats that cover the ears.

I look down the humongous mountain we will now have to descend with the brakes on all the way as I hold my heart for dear life. *Down the rabbit hole!*

At the base, we pull onto the main street of Huancayo, a town you could have missed if you sneezed. The bustling main street is crowded with a flock of scrawny birds and a handful of anorexic cows wandering about aimlessly. My father points out a few landmarks on the side while we drive into town.

"There, right there. Remember, Rosy, that's where I beat the daylights out of that little... well he was asking for it. And there that is where me and Chucho used to pick up all the girls!" His face lights up as he looks at the main plaza. "Oh wow. It's been such a long time... such a very long time."

We pile out of the van when we hit the main plaza. The mini-park has a few green sprouts of grass and a small bridge that is raised above a sad-looking murky pond. I cross the bridge and pause for a second, frozen in time in the middle of the bridge. *CLICK. A picture to remember.* The last picture before he told me the truth about what really happened that day.

"Come on, we can walk to the house from here." Tia Rosy motions to the fatigued group. We leave the van securely locked and parked on the dirt road.

"We're home!" Tia Maruja calls out as we reach a house nestled in the corner.

We are standing in front of a tiny, one-story, lime green concrete house. The front lawn is nicely manicured, while elegant looking iron bars enclose the area. A delicate detailed wood trimming frames the house neatly. My father rings the ancient doorbell located on the concrete pillar that guards the house.

"*!Ah ya llegaron los Yanquis!*" a nicely dressed man calls out as he opens the front door.

"Ady, your cousin Luis, my son," Tia Maruja introduces.

We sit down to the traditional "lonche": tea, milk with coffee, and day old bread. There is small talk about the weather, the economic downfall of the US, and of course soccer.

"We should start unpacking. We are only staying a few days, Luis. This was such a long trip," my aunt explains.

"Come on, I'll show you around the house," Papi motions for me to follow.

Standing in the front living room, he comments, "The kids would hardly ever spend any time here, this was mostly for guests and entertaining." We stick our heads into each of the four modest-sized bedrooms. "Lucy and Rosy's room. Maru and Lillie's room. Lucho, Oso, my room… and Monchi."

Monchi was Papi's younger brother. He and Papi were best friends, they were so close in age that they did everything together. Papi stayed at his bedside and refused to move the whole time Monchi was fighting the fever that eventually took his life. He passed away at age seven. For months after, Papi refused to get out of bed and lost a dangerous amount of weight. The doctors blamed Monchi's death on an unknown precondition. The loss of his brother at such a young age with no explanation was the reason my Tio Lucho went into medicine.

"And this is the central garden. Mamita used to have this looking wonderful with plants here and there. She would order plants to be shipped here from different parts of Peru." We step out of the enclosed garden and onto the other side of the house.

"Wow Papi, this house is beautiful," I marvel.

"It should be, it was built to your grandmother's specifications. Your grandfather built this house for her like the Taj Mahal. He put his heart into this house." He points to the concrete floor we are standing on, and adds, "-and a piece of his heart in the foundation too! Papi had a solid gold pocket watch that his father gave to him when he was a teenager. All the kids used to play with it and joke about who was going to inherit it. The day they laid the concrete for the foundation he was up on a ladder and as he bent down to grab something, PLOP, it fell into the concrete mix. The workers all scrambled to retrieve it, but him being the sentimental person he was, he told them to leave it. 'So that a piece of me will always be here with the family in the house I built for them.'"

I was standing in a house built for me. He didn't even know I was ever going to exist but he built this house with all of his soon to be children and grandchildren in mind. These walls are a cocoon for the Yllanes-Luza clan who are spread out all over the world. I traveled so very far to come home to a house I never laid eyes on. A house built for me by a man who loved me even before I came into this world.

"*Who are you?*"

"*I hardly know, sir, just at present-at least I know who I was when I got up this morning, but I think I must have changed several times since then.*"

The Land of Piru

The original name for butterfly was "flutterby". The original name for Peru as the indigenous population of Panama called it was Piru, meaning "land of abundance" in Quechua. Not to be confused with the Piru Street Boys from Compton, the umbrella street gang alliance under the larger alliance, the Bloods. True, both indigenous Peruvians and Piru Street Boys were not forces to be reckoned with. The Street Boys and the people of the Incan Empire both were determined to protect their neighborhood from outsiders. History would have turned out very different if the people of the Incan Empire were as strapped as the Piru Street Boys.

Ladies and Gentlemen,

A totally fictional reenactment of the Battle of Cajamarca featuring the Piru Street Boys:

Atahualpa hears tales of white bearded men approaching his territory. Atahualpa sends messengers with presents to Pizarro and his men in an attempt to have them leave in peace. Seeing the riches, Pizarro refuses to leave and requests a meeting with Atahualpa. A few days later Pizarro strategically places his men around the area where they are to meet in Cajamarca. Atahualpa strolls in with a crew of 7,000 unarmed soldiers and attendants. The friar speaks to them about the precepts of the Catholic religion which quickly loses its meaning with a poorly equipped translator. After this sorry explanation, the friar hands Atahualpa a Bible stating that he and his people should immediately convert or become an enemy of the church and the Spanish Crown.

Atahualpa scoffs and questions "Where you get your authority from, who you roll with?"

The friar, deeply offended, points to the Bible, "He is my authority, fool!"

Atahualpa grabs the heavy Bible and shakes it close to his ear, "Why then don't he speak to me bitch?" tossing it to the ground.

Pizarro, in retaliation for such disrespect, executes Atahualpa's 12-man honor guard and takes Atahualpa hostage in return for a hefty ransom.

FREEZE ~

In real history this is where Spanish troops massacre 2,000 of Atahualpa's crew. The Spanish troops with their horses, guns and steel swords, helmets and armor, a juggernaut against the unarmed Inca forces sporting only their leather armor. This was the start of the end of the Incan empire.

REWIND ~

Had the Piru Street Boys been present at the Battle of Cajamarca...

From behind the looming mountain appear a mob of heavily armed Piru Street Boys riding in on various low riders wielding a nice assortment of deadly doodads. Firing shots into the air as they ride up, bodies hanging out the windows, they yell battle cries. The grandmaster of the Street Boys steps calmly out the passenger's seat of a burgundy Chevy Nova, its hood adorned with an elaborate painting of the sun. The passenger door sports an elegant Old English tag "Pimps in Red Uniforms".

"Is there a problem here?" he gestures towards Pizarro, with a switchblade to the bound Atahualpa.

"This fool doesn't seem to be cooperating with us," Pizzaro retorts, perched high on his horse.

"What are you pushing?" the arrogant grandmaster throws out, while spitting on the ground Pizzaro is nervously trying to keep.

"These uncivilized heathens need some savin'. It won't cost them a damn thing to renounce their gods and walk in the path of the Lord."

"I think... that you are the one that needs savin' right now," he says with a sinister smile. He walks slowly towards Atahualpa, using a switchblade to free him from the ropes that bind him. Pizarro's guards cowardly look the other way. The two leaders exchange a cryptic handshake and with hands interlocking, the grandmaster gracefully swings Atahualpa full force onto Pizzarro's horse.

Atahualpa lets out a menacing cry before he slits Pizarro's throat. Pushing his limp body off the horse, he charges towards Pizarro's army with a small Glock. By this time Pizarro's troops have already retreated, pissing themselves with fear. The unlucky ones that are too slow to escape are rewarded with a full force beat down by the Piru Street Boys. Fists flying, knives gashing, and guns-a-popping, the battle finishes before it has even begun.

The Battle of Cajamarca has been unanimously won by Atahualpa with the alliance of the much-to-be-feared Piru Street Boys. The Spanish forces quickly retreat to their side of the ocean in the upcoming days as if they never stepped foot on the land. The power, gold, and silver stay with their rightful owners, forever changing the future and economic stability of Peru, better known now as the land of Piru.

Papi is playing with a tiny switchblade he found in the garden. "When we were kids we used to play marbles with blades. See who could fling it the farthest with the blade on the sidewalk. Stick ball with some unfortunate mother's broom. We would cut out the tongues of the shoes and make slingshots. Oohh there were a million things to do and we didn't need much to do it. Toy stores didn't exist back then, the toy stores were here." he points to his head with the blunt part of the switchblade.

We stayed in Huancayo for a few days, exhausting absolutely everything there was to do in the tiny little town. It was time to make our way to our next destination, Tarma. As we say our goodbyes, I also bid a silent farewell to the home that my grandfather built.

Passing the huge bronze statue of Pizarro in the main plaza, we work our way to the bottom of the other side of the mountain.

"Oh, Ady, before we leave look there to the right. That is where your mother used to live." Tia Rosy gestures with a cigarette in her hand.

I turn to see a tall ugly brick wall adorned with barbed wire. Papi stops the car so I can look at the wall. *Maybe...*

"Uh, wait, I'll be right back," I say quickly before anyone can stop me. There is a magnetic force calling me to the home. I reach the horrid structure and the camouflaged door. There is a deadly looking doorbell to the side that I press despite the vision I have of being violently electrocuted.

A tiny, brown-faced girl with big dark brown eyes comes to the heavy iron door. She is sporting dirty flip flops with a matching dingy t-shirt and a long skirt.

She looks at me with questioning eyes. *"¿Si buenos días... puedo ayudarte señorita?"*

I explain to her in my halting Spanish that I am from the United States. That my mother lived here a long time ago and I was wondering if I could see the house that she grew up in.

She looks at me suspiciously, then looks behind me at the van packed with my family. With accusing eyes, she replies in Spanish, "No, I don't think I can do that, no one is home but me. So very sorry young lady."

Before she slams the door on me I am able to catch a glance inside. The front yard is a big plot of dirt devoid of any lovely grassy patches or plants. The structure of the house itself looks like it is made out of clay; a layer of dirty, grimy, brown earth. I assume that a wooden shack in the corner is the outhouse Mami mentioned a few times, the one that Tia Gladys fell into when she was a toddler that caused her to be deaf in one ear. The simple-looking home is dreary and not at all what I was expecting. I knew Mami grew up in poverty in a third world country, but it is a shock for me to see exactly how third world it really was. I thought it ironic that this land was considered the land of abundance when it seems like the majority of Peruvians didn't have a pot to piss in. Abundant in what, I ask myself, disillusioned as I make my way to the van packed with my family.

Brainless Giants

Brazil got its name from the nut, not the other way around. The full name of Los Angeles is actually "El Pueblo de Nuestra Señora la Reina de Los Ángeles del Rio de Porciúncula". Santa Ana de la Ribera de Tarma, the Pearl of the Andes, Tarma for short, is where my father is from. It is warmly nestled within the mountain ranges of the Andes Mountains. Like a rollercoaster ride, the descent down the looming mountain into the valley of the city of Tarma is exhilarating. At first glance the scenic view of Tarma knocks you out and makes you take a nap, it really is that tranquil. The laid-back, sleepy scenery is similar to running through a field of poppies (close eyes, form a mental picture of Dorothy, the Cowardly Lion, Tin Man, and the Scarecrow running to the gates of the Emerald City).

"We are almost theerree!!" Tio Pepe shouts excitedly, rubbing his hands together. He is getting auto fever. For the last few hours he looked like he was going to jump out of the van. You can't stick a cartoon character in a car for hours on end; the ink melts after a while.

"Sweet Tarma!" my grandmother exclaims while tugging at my hand in her ice cold grip.

We pull up to an enormous stone building sitting on the corner of a very beautiful, quiet neighborhood. We all crawl out of the van, everyone groaning, cracking, and stretching at the same time. We enter a large empty storefront through a tiny hidden door.

"This is part of the house too. Your mother and I used to sell a variety of things here. Lamps, light bulbs, plants, food... not much of a theme to the store now that I think about it. We didn't... have it open very long anyways..." Papi trails off, putting his head down as if he forgot something as he makes his way to a backroom. The air turned stale and tight all of a sudden, like everyone was holding their breath at the same time.

"Let's grab our things and bring them upstairs," Tia Lucy calls out, breaking the awkward silence that seems to have come out of nowhere.

As I grab my book bag from the van, I look down the long narrow street at a mother running full force with her baby in hand trying to catch an already departed bus. I slam the heavy metal door behind me, not realizing it would be a long while before I step foot outside to see daylight again.

The house itself looks like a small apartment complex. My father explains, as we make our way up to where we would be staying, that the once enormous one family house had now been parceled off into many smaller residences. The main part of the original house was still kept in the family and is presently being occupied by Mamita's sister, Tia Carmen.

"Ah welcome, welcome my little ones!" Tia Carmen calls out thunderously as we make our way into the house. "Long trip, I bet you are all starving, need to rest your weary feet! Long trip, long trip," she calls out as she ushers us inside.

Carmencita was born in 1821 in an open field on a stormy summer night (no, not really but she looks that old). She is sporting tan Skippies with bright red dress pants and a yellow furry blouse. I wonder if old age triggers colorblindness. I also wonder if she noticed she forgot to put in her teeth this morning. Her cheeks are bright red with a huge red nose to match. Her comical appearance matches her sassy personality.

Walking around, we can tell there are plenty of empty rooms for us to pick from.

"Adelita you can take this room! This was your great grandparents' room. Everything just as it was back then, not much changed in this room!" Carmencita calls out.

I step into the room and feel a warm breeze come in from the window that sits very high on the wall. I put my things on the mahogany carved bed as I inspect the bedroom. The walls are made of stone, concrete, gingerbread, something like that, I'm not a mason I really have no idea. The only attempt at decorations is a huge framed portrait of my grandmother's mother. I know it is her because of the tales everyone told about her being fair skinned with blue eyes. The portrait is one of those old reproductions printed back when color photos were the newest thing; the ones that look like a child took a black and white picture and painted the main parts with watercolors. She sits on a chair with her hands folded in front of her, brilliantly blond, bold blue eyes, oval face, wearing a pearl necklace and a lace blouse. The giant silver frame is now tarnished with age. I look in the mirror above the dresser behind me at my long black hair, dark brown eyes, round face, plaid shirt, baggy jeans, and Nikes.

This is the last stop on our journey before we return to Lima. With a knot in my stomach, I decide to stay as far away from Papi for as long as I can on this leg of the trip. *Ignorance is bliss.* I rest my spinning head on the huge bed for a moment and fall asleep.

According to myth, the creator god Viracocha rose from Lake Titicaca in Peru, coming during the time of darkness to bring forth light. He is represented as wearing the sun for a crown, thunderbolts in his hands, and tears descending from his eyes as rain. He created the sun, the moon, and the stars. He created mankind by breathing into huge stones, but his first attempt were brainless giants that displeased him. So he destroyed them with a great flood and made better ones with smaller stones.

Content with his creations, he eventually disappeared across the Pacific and never returned. It is said that he wandered the earth disguised as a beggar teaching his new creations the basics of civilization.

I can't find my way, I can't see the road before me and I don't know where I am. I need a guiding light, all I see is darkness. Where are you? Viracocha!

I vaguely remember seeing my father at my bedside. A flash of Mamita's worried frown. Why is she crying? What the hell is that horrible monotonous noise? It's giving me a headache. It feels like giants stomping on my head. I feel the darkness and deafening silence. I call out for him but no sound comes out.

When I open my eyes I am wrapped up in a million heavy blankets and there is a huge bowl by my bedside. I feel like I have been trampled by a drunken elephant. I'm in my pajamas and I smell horrible. I try to climb out of bed but I'm paralyzed. I look up to see a small black cat sitting on the high windowsill. He is staring at me as if to see what I am going to do next. I try calling out but still nothing comes out. I grab a spoon from the bedside and bang it on the ceramic bowl on the nightstand.

Mamita flies into the room with a pile of laundry still in her hands. "*Ay chiquitita*, you are awake!! We are so happy you are okay. How do you feel? Do you want some hot tea? Something to eat? A shower perhaps?"

"I'm hungry," I barely manage to choke out.

Papi walks in with a worried look. "Hey there *princessa*. Are you okay? You gave us a little scare."

I stare at him with a questioning look, nodding my head and shrugging my shoulders.

"Carmencita had a group of her friends over here for nights praying by your bedside. You were fighting off something ugly. You had a high fever, puking, diarrhea, cold sweats. There is nothing left inside you!" he says, fidgeting with a tissue in his hands.

I was in and out of consciousness with severe stomach issues. If you have ever had food poisoning you know how much you feel like you are knocking at death's door. The excruciating pain and unfathomable discomfort are indescribable. Almost as bad as the sickness, is the medication they give you so that you don't die of dehydration. "*Suero*", some kind of deadly serum, tastes like a very dangerous toxic liquid... nothing. Try to imagine a mouthful of liquid nothing. Sounds weird, but it is the worst taste in the world. Now, I recall the near-death experience that I battled. I was hallucinating also, I remember as I look for the black cat next to the empty closed window. I had been cleansed of everything I had in me. I was quite literally a new person after that excruciating ordeal.

We were never able to pinpoint the deadly culprit that I ingested. Weak and not able to do much I stay in bed all day eating the universal stomach remedy, J-E-L-L-O. I lounge in my great grandparents' massive bed looking at old photo albums that Carmencita brings to me every so often. I am lying in a bed of memories when Papi walks in.

"Do you need anything?" I am barely able to shake my head. "You were out for almost a week. When you feel up to it we should be heading back to Lima. So just let me know... and then we just have to stop one place here in Tarma before we head back. Okay... well... just let me know." he says softly as if he were to speak too loud he would accidently tell me the truth then and there.

"Where?" I try not to sound scared as I ask the question, but my voice quavers and it gives me away. I'm afraid of what my father might say, and where he might take me next.

Moshe

You are now turning the page as you sit in your bed under the blankets reading, or as you wipe the sand off the pages while lounging on the beach. If you're an avid reader, you are looking at the lower right hand corner for the page number. We are nearing the end of an average novel (unless you are a muggle reading Harry Potter). You are glancing at the quantity of pages left before you reach the back cover (not too many). You don't have to be Sherlock Holmes to tell that we are nearing the end.

The end of my history, my history of numbers:

We are on page **215** + my parents divorced when I was 7 + I moved to Peru when I was **16** + my next milestone will happen when I am **27 = 265, 2+6+5 = 13**.

13. Triskaidekaphobia is the fear of the number 13. The Last Supper seated twelve disciples and Christ, forming a group of thirteen to share in his last meal. Friday the 13th, 1307 was the date the assembly of the Knights Templar were systematically assassinated. Naughty number 13, or in some instances Not-So-Bad 13. In Sikhism, the number 13 is considered a special number since 13 is *tera* in Punjabi, which also means "yours" (as in, "I am yours, O Lord"). In Egypt, there are thirteen steps on the ladder that leads to eternity. Upon the thirteenth step it is said that the soul reaches the source of itself and attains spiritual completion.

I barely have strength the next day to get up for breakfast. As I get dressed I notice my jeans drooping off my frail waist. I lost serious weight during my involuntary cleansing fest here in Tarma. I enter the dining room where the French doors are left open, revealing a beautiful mahogany dining table with elaborately carved chairs. These are finely handcrafted furnishings you can't purchase nowadays.

"Good morning," I greet as I make my way around the table. Each of the twelve seats around the table is occupied as I sit down. *13 of us.*

"So Adelita, how are you feeling?" Tio Pepe questions. "I bet you didn't miss that back molar that I pulled while you were knocked out?"

I search my back teeth with my tongue for a gap. Finding all of them in place I give a weak laugh. He *is* a dentist, after all.

"Ah I feel… lighter, I guess. I think I need to eat for a few days continuously to catch up." I tug at the waist of my baggy jeans to create the full effect.

"Oh here," Mamita says as she pushes a plate of scrambled eggs, fruit and toast towards me. I kill my food and quickly serve myself seconds.

"Ah she eats like her father!" Carmencita remarks. "Your father would sit at this dinner table with all his brothers and sisters and not get up until he finished everyone else's scraps. Lucho didn't like beans. Maru would throw him her broccoli. Lucy despised red meat so she would switch plates with him when he finished his. Oso would make little packages of carrots and roll it over to your father down the table when Abuelita wasn't looking."

"I don't like to see food go to waste. I'm a barrel without a bottom," Papi remarks, popping a grape in his mouth. "Ah, but nobody knew my name when Easter would come around. Abuela would set the table with homemade candies, cookies, and cakes. A sugary feast for each one of us on our placemat at the table. All the kids from the youngest to the oldest would be anxious to get into the dining room that morning. Then Abuelo would open those doors and let in the rush of screaming kids. Ah, no, on that day Moises would not be bombarded with flying napkins filled with sweets. True?" He tells the story with the same liveliness in his eye that he always gets when he reminisces about his childhood.

As Papi tells his tale, I can see the room we are sitting in fill with giggles, love, and family. A room nicely packed with blissful memories. Like ghosts, the phantom visions of my family as children vanish when Mamita touches me lightly on the shoulder.

"We are going to leave tomorrow and start our journey back to Lima. Today we will be visiting my mother and father to pay them tribute. The church is going to hold a mass in their names to honor the anniversaries of each of their departures."

As we finish breakfast, I help clear the table then run upstairs to get ready. Tia Rosy walks in, and asks, "I was wondering if you brought any church clothes? I didn't, I wasn't planning on going to a mass on this excursion."

"No, I don't have any church clothes, just my jeans, t-shirts, and a bikini." I reply with a frown, while gesturing to my suitcase on the floor.

"Maybe we can find something in here," she suggests as she opens the huge armoire next to my suitcase.

Tia Rosy pulls out a few outdated dresses and crisp long skirts. "Your great grandmother was a very petite lady. She was a tiny person with a big personality, very determined for the times in which she was living."

I sort through the vintage clothes and decide on the least old-lady-like blouse and matching skirt I can find. After I change, I go to the room where Mamita is staying.

"Mamita, do you have any shoes I can wear?" I ask as I crawl into her bed.

"Mmmm. I don't usually carry shoes for a whole army with me, I only have two feet. But I think I might have a pair of sandals I brought along that would look nice on you. Let me check," she replies as she searches in her suitcase, which is resting on the foot of the bed. She finds a chocolate and hands it to me as she remarks, "Almost ready my dear."

She turns her back to me and looks in the mirror to put her earrings on. "I want you to remember that sometimes things are better unsaid. Sometimes pain never goes away, it just gets dull with time. The love that parents have for a child is one that you will not be able to comprehend until you have one of your own. When you do, then you will know that everything you do from then on is for the sake of your child." She hands me a pair of golden sandals as she adds, "Oh and of course for your grandchildren as well." She gives my head a little nuzzle with her cold nose, and slips a pearl necklace into my hand.

I nod, though I am not really sure what she is referring to as I slip on the golden sandals and the pearl necklace. As we all spill out into the street on our way to the church, the sun blinds me for a moment.

Remember those series of books in the 80's called Choose Your Own Adventure? You would be the main character in the book with a great adventure on the rise and all of a sudden the page would break.

~Reader you can choose to take the path to the right into the jungle to search for the lost treasure of Nabooti facing danger, malaria, and wild animals on the way by turning to page 53 or go left to the plane that is waiting to bring you back safely to your home in England, by turning instead to page 24. Then you would quietly look around, read ahead and check to see what option would be better.

~Reader you can choose one of two paths for Ady to follow:

Option 1: Let Ady climb into the van with her family to the church where she is going to eventually learn about the secret that her father has been keeping from her all of these years, possibly changing her entire existence as she knows it.

Option 2: Let Ady go to the nearest corner to take the microbus that is on its way to Mancora, a beach resort town in northwestern Peru known for its attractive turquoise beaches and warm waters where she will be able to sprawl out on the pristine sand with a virgin margarita in one hand and an anticucho in the other, possibly having the greatest day of her life as she knows it.

You have picked Option 1: (Damn you!) Please proceed.

Regaining my vision from the blinding sun, I reluctantly retreat into the van. Within a few short minutes, we are at the tiny church tucked away on a side street of Tarma. The bells are loudly ringing above us as we enter a church adorned with thousands of dollars' worth of statues and stained glass windows. It looks like it was plucked right off the streets of Rome and plunked in the middle of the Peruvian poverty in Tarma.

The mass itself is a basic service, all the same prayers that I now know by heart in Spanish. At the very end of the mass is where the priest makes a special announcement about Julio Moisés Luza Otazú and his wife, Juana Felícita Ortiz Gonzáles del Riego.

I look down and realize that my palms are sweaty and my heart has been beating a mile a minute for the whole mass. I am bracing myself for the priest to announce, "And let us pray for Adeline Yllanes in this time of uncertainty. Let us pray for her and for the parents who left her on the doorstep of the Yllanes household, in a wicker basket, 16 years ago."

During the part of the mass when you are to shake hands with the people seated around you and say "Peace be with you", I suspiciously look at a young married couple behind us and wonder if they are there to meet me and tell me they are my biological parents.

"Let us go outside," Mamita suggests, holding my hand.

As we make our way outside to the back of the church, we encounter what looks to be a massive maze. There are rows and rows of colossal white pillars about eight feet high. I walk over to one, curious about what they could possibly be. As I get closer, I make out a name plate with the year of birth and death. *Hundreds of tombs*. I am used to the kind of dead bodies that are discreetly hidden out of site, in the earth below. I am surprised at this new realm of crypt keeping.

I brush my finger across the bumpy white stucco. *Intriguing*. I never enjoyed the idea of being trapped underground upon my death. I am semi-claustrophobic and just the idea of being compacted by hundreds of pounds of dirt (even if I wasn't breathing any longer) leaves me terrified. I want to be cremated, have my sister mix the ashes with paint and have her paint me into lovely beach scenery. I can then hang on my grandchild's mantel indefinitely.

"These have been here for hundreds of years and they still look new," Papi comments, walking up behind me so quietly he startles me. "Like the dead have a way of rejuvenating their burial places. You know, there are at least ten people in each burial chamber. They put them in, wait, and then push the bones back. They are separated only by a slab of stone."

"Nice," I reply, cringing at the thought of lying for eternity among smelly strangers.

We walk for a few minutes until we reach the middle of the cemetery.

"This is where my parents are resting," Mamita says to me as everyone gathers around. There is a small copper cone next to the name plates where Tia Rosy places water and a few red flowers. Mamita places her palm on the name plates next to the compartment. Everyone bows their heads and she begins a prayer as she holds her rosary. *I wish I could have met them.*

"We have a few more tombs to visit." Tia Lily motions for me to follow.

On the other side of the very same crypt where Mamita's parents are, on almost the same level as them, is another tomb. The nameplate is worn and barely legible, and reads: Raul Bruno Yllanes Monje.

"This is your cousin Brunito. He was my first born, passed away suddenly before he turned a year old." Tia Lily informs me with half a smile. "I miss him terribly but I rest easily knowing that he is well accompanied up there... and also here as well." She gives me a kiss on the forehead and points to the name below her son's. As she walks away she grabs Papi's hand and pushes him closer to me, leaving Papi and me alone at the tomb.

I take a closer look at the engraved name:

"Moshe Yllanes-Alvarez *~10 de octubre 1971 ~ 11 de noviembre 1971"*

Just a baby.

"Mama, I've been wanting to tell you for a long time now," Papi says in English.

Playing Sapo in the Clouds

The little boy that once pass by my life like a swift kiss. Mami didn't even know that she was pregnant when he decided to snuggle and grow in my mother's womb. She was young and inexperienced at the age of 20. The medical diagnosis came from Mamita one day, "Anita you are pregnant my dear, it is time for you to go see a doctor." She must have had that pregnancy glow.

Mami and Papi were ecstatic with the news about their first baby to be. He was named Moshe after Moshe Dayan, the Israeli military warrior who was a crusader for peace. He came into this world born a leader with a knack for making his followers smile and obey his every demand. He was proudly adorned with hand knit blankets from adoring aunts. Moshe was a content baby that ate, laughed, and slept sporting a serene smile.

My parents were just waking up, early in the morning, in the little back-room apartment behind the storefront in Tarma. Mami woke up to feed the baby, when, to her horror, she saw he was not breathing. No screaming, no cries for help, just a helpless plea as she turned to a still sleeping Papi. She violently shook him awake, pleading with her eyes to fix the baby that was now limp in her arms. Without a word they both frantically threw on their robes, Mami stepping into her golden slippers. They rushed out, leaving the front door open as their small black cat wandered out into the street, leaving him to cry for help.

Running down the long narrow street full force with her baby in hand they reached the local clinic in desperation where the hopelessness set in. "My baby is not moving, please help me, he is not moving!" Mami pleaded as she handed Moshe to a nurse. That would be the last time that she held her little angel in her arms. He was rushed to the back, while Mami dropped to her knees, empty open arms waiting for him to come back.

"Your mother used to tell me that she felt like she was in a cloud. She couldn't see anything but the image of Moshe for a while," Papi murmurs as he takes a long drag of his cigarette. "She didn't smile anymore, just spent most of her time with Mamita trying to hide from the loss. I was devastated myself, but maybe I think it is different when a mother loses a child. She had a bond with Moshe, 9 months before I met him. I didn't know how to make her better. Time, time, was the only thing that made her come back to reality."

I asked Mami about Moshe years later and she smiled and cried, "It was the first time in my life that I felt something was mine that I created, and that was taken away from me that day."

"Oh Papi. I didn't know... I didn't think that you were going to tell me... I'm so sorry. I thought you were going to tell me something else. I feel terrible that happened to you and Mami. I can't imagine... but what happened, was he sick? Was the baby sick?" I ask all my questions with a heavy heart.

"They never did tell us what happened, exactly. Back in those days, it was custom to lay babies on their bellies to prevent stomach discomfort. He was tightly wrapped and on his belly that morning. We can speculate about what happened, but we don't know for sure. Your mom didn't want to forget Moshe but she wanted to lock away that pain. That's why we never mentioned him to you or your brothers. I'm sorry we kept it from you for such a long time, but I did want you to come see him, since we made this trip to Peru. I want you to realize that there is much more to you than what you see in your hand. Your roots are deep and your branches need to grow even longer to compensate." he says as he walks away.

I turn to the crypt that shelters my older brother. My world suddenly seems to double in size as if I am not the center of the universe any longer. There was history before I came into this world and there will be history yet to be written after I leave. Moshe was on this earth only but a month, but he was able to leave a footprint in the path that my parents walked. I had chances that he didn't and I didn't seem to be going too far with what I was given.

Hello there brother. I'm your little sister, Ady. Do you understand me as I speak to you or are you located in the part of the sky where they speak Spanish? How do you spend your days up there? Do you play sapo with the Care Bears up there? Do you get bored up there? Do you send the rain down here or do you get wet too? When I look up after the rain stops and there is a sliver of sunlight beaming through the clouds, is that you? I never met you but I bet we would have loved each other very much. Hello there brother, my name is Ady and we have never met, but I know you will always be a part of me that I carry like a little treasure in my pocket.

My Book of Life

Pop quiz, quick, what is Mozart's older sister's name? In her younger days she received top billing. She was an equally talented if not arguably a better musician than her ugly brother. As she grew older, however, the views of her parents and society at the time made it nearly impossible for her to continue her career any further. Amadeus was lucky as hell that she was born missing one critical body part, otherwise he might have been cast to the shadows. This, sadly, can be an analogy for the portrayal of Peru and the United States; the brother born with the infamous big Webster's dick...tionary. The fame and overt popularity of the United States has greatly overshadowed the talent and wonders of Peru. By the way, her name was Maria Anna, born to Anna Maria Mozart. *Anna Maria... my mother's name.*

It was a great relief to me when I learned that the huge secret that had been kept from me didn't rip my roots out from the shaky ground I was resting on. I felt liberated that I was still able to have ownership of the Yllanes name, while at the same time sad to learn about the life that was lost such a long time ago. I had an older brother who would forever be the image of a baby in my mind. The paperwork that I saw my first day of class that listed 3 children born with Peruvian nationality now made more sense, and no longer made me question my origin. I never revealed to my father my suspicions about being adopted. As he is reading this now he is probably shaking his head and laughing, while munching on a handful of peanuts in his mouth instead of a cigarette, which he has hopefully quit for good by the time this is published. Yes Papi, your silly daughter thought she was adopted for a while.

Almost 15 years later, as I reminisce through my photo albums about my days in Peru, I come across two pictures. On one side is a picture of my grandmother's mother, a copy of the same photograph that was hanging in the house in Tarma. The other side is a picture of me sitting on a chair in the veranda of the same house, the night before we left for Lima. My great-grandmother and I are sitting in the same exact chair on the same porch, with our hands folded in front of us. We are wearing the same lace blouse, the one I found hidden in her armoire that day we went to the cemetery, and the same pearl necklace. Both our feet are crossed at the ankles, adorned with golden slippers. The only disparity, the only thing that makes us distinctly different, is that I am smiling.

Like I mentioned before, this is not an after school special. I don't suddenly realize at the age of 16 what the meaning of life is. This stage of my life is a step in the direction of falling off that cliff and realizing that life on this earth is just a short journey. A first realization that you are the only one that creates your own reality. Nobody was going write my book of life for me.

However, during my time in Peru I did realize that the figment of my imagination that I grew up with was really a magnificent reality. The powerhouse where my family is from is stuff that legends are made of. The Incan Empire encompassed thousands of square miles. It was populated with audacious architectural engineers and filled with elaborate farming terraces, canals, and drainage systems. We were long ago skilled in fine art and music. Our people were pioneers in high quality craftsmanship in pottery, sculpture, and textiles. Incas constructed stone temples without mortars that fit together so well one could not fit a knife through the stonework.

In the sixteenth century, the Incas controlled more territory than any other country in South America. Yes, *your reign was short like leprechauns*. The Inca Empire's relatively short reign did not hinder its imposing imprint in Peruvian history and beyond. During its two-year rule between 1531 and 1533, the Inca was able to administer a full-fledged civilization complete with an overall ruler, several bureaus, an official language, and a universal religion. *Try fitting that inscription onto a trophy.* The oldest city in the Americas, the ancient pyramids of Caral, predate the Inca civilization by 4,000 years. It is the biggest and most impressive example of monumental architecture where 3,000 people thrived in 2627 B.C.

Our oversea excursion ended a little over a year after we moved to Peru. Papi had no luck finding employment and I had a permanent stamp on my forehead that read, "Made in America." We moved back to West Hartford where I attended Conard High School again with a newfound admiration for what I was given. I proudly brought back with me a colossal chunk of my family tree that I never knew existed. *Now try to declare that on a customs form: Big Ass Tree.*

I came back with the curtain no longer shielding my eyes to the reality that I lived. I never used the term "I'm starving." so loosely again. I never left any uneaten food on my plate or had the audacity to throw away food. I spoke a little louder when someone asked where my family was from. I lost the urge to clarify where Peru has long been located. I didn't see the importance of having the latest Air Force Ones in the newest color anymore. I looked at my recreational drug use through the eyes of the street children of Lima.

My path was slowly clearing of all the debris that cluttered my road to what was yet to be written. My father was fortunate enough to secure a job and was able to nurse his broken heart with time. My mother was plucked violently from the crumpled wreckage of her car by Buddha and placed gingerly on the other side of the street. With the aid of singing Tibetan bowls and the chiming of tiny bells, she was able to meditate her way back to rediscover the mom that I grew up with. Unfortunately, my little sister Chiara, would not walk away from Mami's battle unscathed. She suffered wounds while I was away that she would have to carry with her while she rode her bike across the world in search of *her* treasure.

Sadly, I myself would also undergo unforeseen and debilitating wounds in my life. It's funny how tiny decisions can actually change the course of your future. If only I hadn't jumped into his Cadillac that day on Arch Street in New Britain at the age of seventeen, when he asked me if I needed a ride home from work...

I couldn't find the baby. I felt deaf and blind searching the bed and the floor for any sign of her. Blood everywhere; I didn't know where it was coming from. Was it mine... his... the baby's? I felt like I was going to be sick. Wake up, it's just another nightmare! As I fell into unconsciousness I heard someone screaming a haunting, sad, wailing scream. I didn't realize, as everything went black, that it was me.

I am NOT, nor have I ever been: a man, a lesbian, handicapped, famous, a child soldier of war, a rape survivor, Jewish, rich, homeless, Indian, Muslim, a movie star, adopted, poor, abused, blind, the President of the United States, schizophrenic, overweight, blonde, incarcerated, a holocaust survivor, uneducated, vegan.

I am.

A Little About the Author

Adeline Yllanes was born in New England in 1980 to two Peruvian parents. She came out of the womb wrapped in a blanket made of newspaper. The ink on the headlines soaked into her skin and she has been dreaming up and emanating words from her soul ever since. She grew up with a trail of alphabets constantly following her wherever she went. The phonetic parade followed her to college where she completed her undergraduate degree in Psychology and her Masters in Student Development in Higher Education at Central Connecticut State University. Her rainbow of rhymes shone above her on her wedding day when she married her high school sweetheart. She currently spends all day at work typing away words in a whirlwind while helping adult students reach their goal of obtaining a college degree. She enjoys traveling with her family and two young daughters, Aymara (Google this name) and Cayana (Google Image this name), around the world. She has traveled to Peru, Spain, Mexico, Puerto Rico, Costa Rica, Virgin Islands, Cuba, Ghana, Japan and Canada. She is currently trying to perfect her gardening and sewing skills. She loves words so much that she vowed not to eat any animals with vowels in their name for as long as she is alive. After publishing her book she vows to travel to Peru and visit Machu Picchu again, climb to the highest point possible to dramatically throw a copy off the side so that her words can fly to where they first originated.

Synopsis of the Book

I want people to know our culture so that my children's children don't forget theirs. When I wrote this book I wanted to write about the journey I took when I was sixteen to live in Peru. My parents made the trip from South America to North America to provide us with better opportunities. I made that journey in reverse as a teenager, moving from where I was raised in Connecticut back to Lima, Peru. The year that I lived there with my family rewarded me with a million reasons why I should make the most out of life in this country I now call home. Publishing this book is one way I can pay homage to my ancestors for providing me with the privilege of that rich experience to mold who I am today; hence, the title of my book, "I Am- Soy".

I would like to point out the concept that the Nigerian author, Chimamanda Ngozi Adichie, covers with her narrative of "The danger of a single story". This is **my** Peruvian-American story, not that of my cousins or even of my brothers and sisters. You cannot read my memoir and now say that you know what it was like for all American born people of Peruvian ancestry growing up in New England. We have many paths and many stories to tell. This was my path and I have written my story. I challenge you to put your story on paper so that the people looking in can have a more accurate frame of reference for who we are and who we can become.

ACKNOWLEDGEMENTS

Thanks to my left hand that showed me my inner peacock and how to make it flourish. You gave me some pretty awesome babies, our mellow mango and the spicy aji amarillo Puti. Girls, I am publishing this book so that you can show your children **where** grandma came from so they can know **who** they come from. To the humble, beautiful radiance that is Mamita, that still shines bright through her children and her grandchildren. To my aunts and uncles in Peru who helped me not walk around the house barefoot and gave this spoiled American unconditional love even when I didn't know how to work a toilet. To the "Nanis" for reading my crap first drafts and pushing me to go out and tell my story. To my mama llama that will probably not talk to me for a few years after she reads this which is going to be awkward because she lives in the house across the street from me. Mark Twain specified that he didn't want his autobiography to be published until 100 years after he passed so as not to offend the living. I am not writing this in vengeance or spite. Our skeletons in the family closet were once living, breathing entities in my youth. Denying the past will not make it unreal for a child dealing with crisis. Don't let your addiction be a prediction of what your future has in store for you. I am- soy, a living breathing product of my experiences growing up and I give thanks to everyone who contributed to that.

Yeah, this book is dedicated to all the teachers that told me I'd never amount to nothin', to all the people …. Uh-ha, it's all good baby bay-bee, uh

Write your story down before it is lost to time.

[signature] 2017

Google Henrietta Lacks